The Multilateral Investment
Guarantee Agency

MIGA and Foreign Direct Investment: Evaluating Developmental Impacts

Gerald T. West and Ethel I. Tarazona

© 1998 The International Bank for Reconstruction
and Development / The World Bank
1818 H Street, N.W., Washington, D.C. 20433

All rights reserved
Manufactured in the United States of America
First printing September 1998

The findings, interpretations, and conclusions expressed in this publication are those
of the authors and should not be attributed in any manner to the World Bank Group,
to its affiliated organizations, or to the members of its Board of Executive Directors
or the countries they represent.

The boundaries, colors, denominations, and other information shown on any
map in this volume do not imply on the part of the World Bank Group any judg-
ment on the legal status of any territory or the endorsement or acceptance of such
boundaries.

The material in this publication is copyrighted. Requests for permission to re-
produce portions of it should be sent to the Office of the Publisher at the address
shown in the copyright notice above. The World Bank Group encourages dissemination of its work and will normally give permission promptly and, when the re-
production is for noncommercial purposes, without asking a fee. Permission to
copy portions for classroom use is granted through the Copyright Clearance Center, Inc., Suite 910, 222 Rosewood Dr., Danvers, Massachusetts 01923, U.S.A.

Gerald West and Ethel Tarazona are staff members of the Guarantees Department
of the Multilateral Investment Guarantee Agency (MIGA).

Cover design by May Eidi.

The photographs on the cover correspond to MIGA evaluated projects and were
taken during the course of monitoring visits. Counter-clockwise: Motorola, Pakistan (background); Banco de Boston housing project, Argentina; Rain Forest Aerial
Tram, Costa Rica; Komatsu, Indonesia; KAFCO, Bangladesh (two pictures); and
AFP Integra, Peru.

Library of Congress Cataloging-in-Publication Data

West, Gerald T., 1944–
     MIGA and foreign direct investment: evaluating developmental impacts / by
  Gerald T. West, Ethel I. Tarazona.
          p.   cm.
     Includes bibliographical references.
     ISBN 0-8213-4346-7 (alk. paper)
     1. Multilateral Investment Guarantee Agency.   2. World Bank—Developing
  countries.   3. Investments, Foreign—Developing countries.   4. Economic development projects—Developing countries.   I. Tarazona, Ethel I.   II. Title
  HG3881.5.W57W47   1998
  332.1'532—dc21

                                                             98-44282
                                                               CIP

Contents

Foreword v

Acknowledgments vi

Abbreviations and Acronyms vii

Introduction ix

I. MIGA's Purpose and Development Mandate

A. The Context 1

B. Agency Growth and Contribution to Development 2

II. MIGA's Evaluation Methodology

A. The Agency's Ongoing Evaluation Efforts 7

B. Selection of Projects for Evaluation 9

C. Selection of Monitoring Officers 9

D. Evaluation Sample 10

E. Project Evaluation Process 12

III. Results on the Ground

A. Introduction 15

B. Verification of Direct Economic Effects 15

C. Types of Developmental Impacts, Conceptual
Framework and Monitoring Findings 17

    1. A Typology of Developmental Impacts 17

    2. Direct Effects 18

        Human Capital Investment 18

        Direct Employment 20

        The Environment 22

    3. Indirect Effects 24

        Upstream and Downstream Effects 24

        Social Development and Poverty Alleviation 28

        Transfer of Knowledge 29

    4. Diffused Effects 30

        The Financial Sector and Capital Markets 30

        Demonstration Effects 32

IV. Case Studies

A. Karnaphuli Fertilizer Company Ltd. (KAFCO), Bangladesh 37

B. Banco de Boston, Argentina 47

C. Crescent Greenwood, Pakistan 59

Conclusions 73

– iii –

Annex:

Projects Evaluated 74

Appendix:

MIGA'S Support of Financial Sector Projects and Their
Contribution to the Development Process 76

MIGA Member Countries 85

Tables:

Table 1 MIGA's Guarantee Portfolio & Developmental Impact,
Fiscal Years 1990–98 3
Table 2 Guarantee Contracts Evaluated 11
Table 3 Selected Developmental Impacts, 25 Evaluated Projects 16
Table 4 Types of Training Provided by MIGA-Assisted Projects 18
Table 5 Summary Table of Developmental Impacts of
25 MIGA-Assisted Projects 34

Figures:

Figure 1 Maximum Contingent Liability, Fiscal Years 1990–98 3
Figure 2 MIGA's Portfolio Outstanding by Region 4
Figure 3 MIGA's Portfolio Outstanding by Sector 4
Figure 4 Active vs. Evaluated Contracts by Region, Fiscal Years 1990–95 11
Figure 5 Active vs. Evaluated Contracts by Industry, Fiscal Years 1990–95 12
Figure 6 Project Evaluation Process 13
Figure 7 Types of Developmental Impacts 17
Figure 8 Number of New Jobs Created, 25 Evaluated Projects 21
Figure 9 KAFCO's Training Program 41
Figure 10 KAFCO's Staff 42
Figure 11 Banco de Boston Mortgage Terms, September 1992 55
Figure 12 Banco de Boston Mortgage Terms, April 1997 55
Figure 13 Banco de Boston Mortgage Program, Employment Generation 56

Boxes:

Box 1 Quality of MIGA's Services 8
Box 2 Investment in Human Capital: SAS Partners/
Gate Gourmet, Turkey 19
Box 3 Environmental Effect: The Rain Forest Aerial Tram, Costa Rica 24
Box 4 Development of Capital Markets: AFP Integra, Peru 32
Box 5 Development Highlights: KAFCO, Bangladesh 38
Box 6 Development Highlights: Banco de Boston, Argentina 51
Box 7 Development Highlights: Crescent Greenwood, Pakistan 63

Foreword

The Multilateral Investment Guarantee Agency (MIGA) was created in April 1988 as a member of the World Bank Group. The Convention establishing MIGA states:

> The objective of the Agency shall be to encourage the flow of investments for productive purposes among members countries, and in particular to developing countries. (Article 2)

To serve this objective, the Agency provides guarantees (or insurance) covering foreign direct investment against the political risks of Transfer Restriction, Expropriation, Breach of Contract, and War and Civil Disturbance in developing member countries. MIGA also carries out advisory and technical assistance to governments of these countries to improve their ability to attract foreign investment. By the end of fiscal year 1998, MIGA had issued 348 guarantees, amounting to about US$4.2 billion in total coverage; the cumulative foreign direct investment facilitated was estimated to be US$25 billion.

The 10th anniversary of MIGA's creation offers an opportunity to take stock of the Agency's accomplishments and its contribution to development. In this respect, it is critically important to measure and assess the impact of MIGA's guarantee activities on the development process, and on the Agency's developmental effectiveness. Since its first project, MIGA has systematically elicited information about the estimated developmental impacts of MIGA-guaranteed investments. These estimates are embodied in the individual guarantee reports conveyed to the Board of Directors before the issuance of a MIGA guarantee, as well as in the Agency's annual reports; the evaluation exercise verified that they have been borne out in reality, in many cases exceeding anticipated results.

This publication, based on several reports made to MIGA's Board of Directors, represents our first attempt to convey to a larger audience MIGA's effort to address the developmental impacts of its guaranteed projects in a comprehensive manner. It is my hope that this publication will help the reader better understand how private foreign direct investment can have a positive effect on the development process, and how MIGA's guarantee activities have directly contributed to that process.

Motomichi Ikawa   August 26, 1998
Executive Vice President
MIGA

Acknowledgments

This report was prepared in MIGA's Guarantees Department. Ms. Aurora Medina Siy and Mr. Edgar F. Restrepo made important contributions for which the authors are deeply grateful. This report was also made possible by the cooperation of the following MIGA officers who conducted project site visits: Mr. Engin Göksu, Mr. Mirghani Hassan, Mr. Roland Pladet, Mr. Robert Rendall, Ms. Houria Sammari, Ms. Patricia Veevers-Carter, Mr. Daniel Wagner, and Mr. Zia Yusuf, and the external consultant, Mr. Michael Stack.

Abbreviations and Acronyms

AFP	Administradora Privada de Fondos de Pensiones
BOT	Build, Own and Transfer
CAS	Country Assistance Strategy
CESCE	Compañía Española de Seguros de Crédito a la Exportación, S.A.
CMO	Collaterized Mortgage Obligations
COFACE	Compagnie Française d'Assurance pour le Commerce Extérieur
COSEC	Companhia de Seguro de Créditos, S.A.
C&L	C&L Deutsche Revision AG
ECGD	Export Credits Guarantee Department
EDC	Export Development Corporation
EID	Export-Import Insurance Division
EPA	Environmental Protection Agency
FDI	Foreign Direct Investment
GDP	Gross Domestic Product
GNP	Gross National Product
IBRD	International Bank for Reconstruction and Development
IDA	International Development Association
IFC	International Finance Corporation
IMF	International Monetary Fund
ISO	International Organization for Standardization
MIGA	Multilateral Investment Guarantee Agency
MITI	Ministry of International Trade & Industry
MT	Metric Tons
NCM	Nederlandsche Credietverzekering Maatschappij N.V.
OeKB	Oesterreichische Kontrollbank Aktiengesellschaft
OND	Office National du Ducroire
OPIC	Overseas Private Investment Corporation
SACE	Sezione Speciale per l'Assicurazione del Credito all' Esportazione
TQM	Total Quality Management
UNDP	United Nations Development Programme

Introduction

MIGA, a member Agency of the World Bank Group, provides political risk insurance to qualified foreign investors in developing member countries and carries out advisory and technical programs for governments of these countries to improve their ability to attract foreign investment. Before issuing an insurance (guarantee) contract, MIGA reviews an investment's eligibility for coverage using criteria established by the MIGA Convention and the Agency's Operational Regulations. One of the essential criteria is the investment's contribution to the development of the host country. Therefore, during the application stage, the Agency systematically gathers information on every prospective investment to assess its economic soundness and its anticipated developmental impact.

There has been increasing interest from the public about the impact of MIGA's insurance activities on development. However, it took some time for MIGA-insured projects to reach a stage where their actual development impact can be evaluated. It is only within the past two years that MIGA has been able to monitor a sufficient number of projects to produce information that could be systematically analyzed and disseminated. Therefore, the purpose of this report is threefold:

- to inform MIGA's shareholders, and the interested public about MIGA's contribution to development;
- to present information on the developmental impact of a sample of 25 MIGA-supported projects that were examined during the first round of the project evaluation; and
- concomitantly, to demonstrate how private sector projects (through foreign direct investment) can have a positive impact on economic development.

Section I of this report describes in broad terms MIGA's development mandate as required by the Agency's Convention and Operational Regulations, and details its progress to enhance its contribution to development. It characterizes MIGA's growth over the last ten years in terms of: membership; cumulative foreign direct investment facilitated in developing member countries; total number of guarantees issued; and the cumulative amount of guarantees issued. This section also illustrates the increasing regional and sectoral diversification of MIGA's portfolio, and presents aggregate statistics about its development effectiveness. Section II provides an overview of the evolution of MIGA's evaluation program and describes its project evaluation methodology and process. Section III verifies quantitative aggregated information about projects' direct economic effects by comparing anticipated development data with actual results retrieved by MIGA staff or independent consultants during the evaluation exercise. Subsequently, the same section supplies evidence of the developmental impacts of MIGA-supported projects following a multidimensional approach that distinguishes between different types of developmental effects. Section IV presents three in-depth case studies: a fertilizer plant in Bangladesh, a denim facility in Pakistan, and a residential mortgage program in Argentina. These case studies served as a basis to test the evaluation framework and to identify further information needs. Finally, the Appendix discusses the special case of the developmental impacts of financial sector investments and the rationale for the support MIGA provides to this type of investment.

I. MIGA's Purpose and Development Mandate

A. The Context

To understand what MIGA means by "developmental effectiveness," it is useful to recall the relevant purposes, constraints, and compromises that are found in MIGA's Convention and Operational Regulations.

MIGA's founders envisaged the creation of a special purpose organization to supplement the activities of the IBRD, the IFC, and other international development finance institutions. To encourage the flow of investment for productive purposes to developing member countries, MIGA was given a mandate to promote investment by providing political risk insurance, and by disseminating information on investment opportunities (Articles 2 and 23 of the Convention). Moreover, MIGA was mandated specifically to complement national and regional investment insurance programs and private insurers (the Preamble and Article 19 of the Convention).

Since its first contract of guarantee, MIGA has sought to ensure that the projects it assists are beneficial to host countries. Conforming to its Convention (Articles 12d(i) and the Operational Regulations (3.05–3.08)), MIGA must satisfy itself that the prospective investment will contribute to the development of the host country before issuing a guarantee (i.e., an insurance contract). MIGA incorporates a summary of the prospective developmental impacts in all President's Reports to the Board and obtains concurrence from MIGA's Board of Directors before issuing a contract of guarantee. MIGA also seeks to complement the IBRD and the IFC by taking into consideration both their broad activities in a country and the specific development objectives contained in the Country Assistance Strategy (CAS).

Since it was designed as a special purpose entity, MIGA was given a modest capitalization and ordered to conduct itself in a financially prudent manner. Article 25 of the Convention states:

> The Agency shall carry out its activities in accordance with sound business and prudential financial management practices with a view to maintaining under all circumstances its ability to meet its financial obligations.

A significant number of constraining parameters were specified in the Convention and the Operational Regulations with respect to how the Agency can offer its guarantees. The Agency was expected to respond swiftly to the applications of prospective private investors. MIGA's Operational Regulations (3.26) call for the Agency to make prompt decisions—to the extent possible within 120 days of receipt of a Definitive Application for a guarantee.

In order to facilitate prompt underwriting decisions, the Operational Regulations (3.27 and 3.28) allow MIGA Staff either to conduct their own assessment of the proposed investment or to rely on a statement by the host government that the pro-

– 1 –

posed investment conforms to the laws, regulations, objectives, and developmental priorities of the country. Given the importance of the developmental impact of prospective investments, MIGA staff has done both, that is, conducted its own assessment and required host country approval for the proposed investments.

Acting as a supplement to other international financial institutions and a complement to other investment insurers, MIGA was expected to facilitate (but not necessarily design) productive private investment in its developing member countries. Unlike institutions providing debt and/or equity financing to a project, investment insurers have considerably less leverage to induce changes in a project's design or implementation. Therefore, like other insurers, MIGA tends to either approve or deny coverage to a foreign direct investment (FDI) in the form that the applicant presents it. (An exception arises wherever a project fails to adequately address potentially significant environmental problems. In such cases, MIGA asks the applicant to modify the project in accordance with the World Bank's policies and guidelines.)

B. Agency Growth and Contribution to Development

Although open only to World Bank member countries, MIGA membership has expanded considerably. In 1988, 42 World Bank member countries subscribed to MIGA's initial capital; 146 countries have since completed membership requirements, which include the signature and ratification of the MIGA Convention and the payment of a capital subscription. Another 18 countries are in the process of joining MIGA as of August 31, 1998.

Since MIGA began operating in the summer of 1989, it has grown into an important catalyst of FDI flows into developing countries. The cumulative FDI facilitated between fiscal years 1990–98 is estimated at US$25 billion. During fiscal years 1990–95, MIGA facilitated (by providing political risk insurance) an annual average FDI of US$1.3 billion. Since then, this average has increased to US$5.7 billion a year. In fiscal 1998 alone, MIGA facilitated about US$6.1 billion in total FDI. This amount exceeds the estimated cumulative FDI facilitated between fiscal years 1990–94 (Table 1).

The guarantee business continues to surge. Since 1990, MIGA has issued 348 guarantees, 55 of them in fiscal 1998. An average of 60 guarantees have been issued annually since 1994. These guarantees have covered investments to and from developing countries. Covered investments have originated in 26 different member countries, seven of which are themselves developing countries: Turkey, Korea, Argentina, Brazil, Saudi Arabia, South Africa, and Uruguay.

Since fiscal 1990, MIGA's guarantee portfolio has risen by an average US$340 million a year and US$450 million since fiscal 1994, net of cancellations and including amounts reinsured. MIGA's maximum contingent liability has grown from US$132 million in the Agency's first year of operations to US$2.8 billion in fiscal 1998; its size has increased almost four times since fiscal 1993 (Figure 1).

With US$830 million in coverage issued in fiscal 1998, MIGA has facilitated FDI in an amount seven times larger since it started operations in 1990. Historically, MIGA has facilitated FDI for more than six times the coverage amount. The cumula-

Table 1. MIGA's Guarantee Portfolio & Developmental Impact, Fiscal Years 1990–98

	FY90	FY91	FY92	FY93	FY94	FY95	FY96	FY97	FY98	Total
Number of guarantees issued	4	11	21	27	38	54	68	70	55	348
Amount of guarantees issued (US$ million)	132	59	313	374	372	672	862	614	830	4,228
Estimated FDI facilitated (US$ billion)	1.0	0.9	0.6	1.8	1.3	2.3	6.5	4.7	6.1	25.2
Estimated number of jobs created	2,700	3,680	2,920	1,720	7,800	8,800	7,200	4,000	8,000	46,820

tive coverage issued reached US$4.2 billion as of the end of fiscal 1998. These guarantees insured a total of 233 new or existing projects, an average of almost 26 projects a year (39 in fiscal 1998).

These projects have had important developmental effects on the host country's economy. An estimated 46,000 jobs have been created directly by the facilitated investments (Table 1). Nevertheless, developmental benefits did not only relate to the creation of jobs. They ranged from directly introducing modern technology, generating foreign exchange earnings, increasing government revenues, and developing local capital markets, to indirectly creating jobs, increasing human capital, and benefiting the surrounding community and project-related businesses. (A more detailed analysis of these development effects is presented in Section III.)

While MIGA's outstanding portfolio of insurance contracts continues to increase in size, it has remained regionally diverse. Figure 2 depicts the regional distribution of MIGA's portfolio in terms of outstanding gross coverage (including reinsurance).

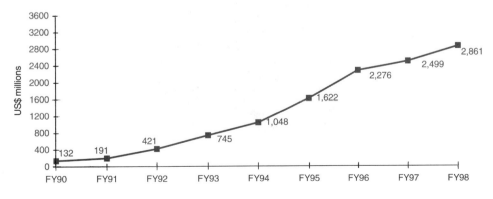

Figure 1. Maximum Contingent Liability, Fiscal Years 1990–98

Figure 2. MIGA's Portfolio Outstanding by Region
(as of June 30, 1998)

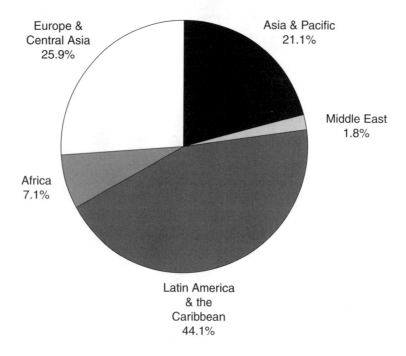

Figure 3. MIGA Portfolio Outstanding by Sector
(as of June 30, 1998)

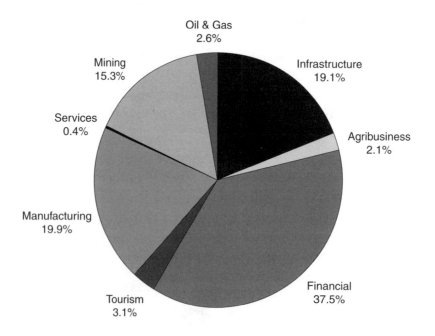

MIGA guarantees have covered investments in 62 different developing member countries. Ten countries received MIGA-supported investments for the first time in fiscal 1998 (seven of which are IDA-eligible[1]): Angola, Bolivia, Cape Verde, Dominican Republic, Equatorial Guinea, India, Kenya, Mozambique, Ukraine, and Uruguay.

As Figure 3 notes, MIGA has facilitated investments in many sectors. MIGA has provided coverage to investments in telecommunications, energy generation, toll roads, hotels, pension funds, leasing, banking, gold mining, and food processing among others. Some previously under-represented sectors have grown considerably in the past six years. In fiscal 1998, 19 percent of the insured investments were in the infrastructure sector, compared to only 1 percent in 1992. The manufacturing sector has grown from 12 percent of the portfolio in fiscal 1992 to almost 20 percent in fiscal 1998.

---

[1] The International Development Association (IDA) is the World Bank Group's concessional lending facility, which concentrates its activities on countries with the lowest per capita income.

II. MIGA'S Evaluation Methodology

A. The Agency's Ongoing Evaluation Efforts

From the very beginning, MIGA has been preparing for evaluating the development effectiveness of MIGA-insured projects by systematically gathering information on the anticipated developmental impacts of each prospective investment. A project's potential developmental impact is an important criterion utilized by MIGA when considering the issuance of a contract of guarantee.

MIGA began in 1993 to develop its evaluation program. During the course of designing the program, the Agency consulted extensively with both the IBRD and the IFC to assure fundamental consonance with the World Bank Group's evaluation practices. However, there was a set of considerations that had to be addressed given the considerable difference existing between project finance operations, such as those in the IBRD and the IFC, and the activities of a political risk insurer (MIGA). Therefore, MIGA relied heavily on the advice of Mr. Mervyn L. Weiner, the first director of the IBRD's Operations Evaluation Staff. In his report to MIGA, Mr. Weiner noted that MIGA, for a variety of reasons, could not adopt wholesale the IBRD's elaborate evaluation procedures. Because of the small size of MIGA's staff, budget, and scale of operations, Mr. Weiner also advised the following:

> A series of periodic development evaluations, largely conducted internally, should be undertaken ... field visits of selected projects by MIGA staff while traveling on other business, and periodic studies of a sample of randomly selected projects plus particularly large or sensitive projects which merit special attention.

MIGA's evaluation methodology was designed to optimize the use of staff time and minimize costs. MIGA also sought to ensure that, as far as possible, the project evaluation process was not too burdensome to the Agency's clients. Mr. Wiener also recommended that MIGA should assess the financial, technical, environmental, economic, and social benefits of its projects, *mainly on the basis of information in sponsors' applications*, it being understood that material misstatement could invalidate future claims" (emphasis added).

Since the start of the MIGA evaluation program, MIGA has carefully followed new methodological developments in the IBRD's and IFC's evaluation and operational analysis programs. The objective has been to benefit from the new methodologies and findings and to assure that MIGA's evaluation program remains as consonant as possible with others in the Bank Group while continuing to take into account the considerable operational differences which exist between MIGA and the other institutions.

A comprehensive evaluation program was implemented in 1996 which outlined several somewhat overlapping phases of MIGA's project and internal operations evaluation program.

– 7 –

Phase I of this program, *Surveying Client Satisfaction*, was completed on schedule in 1996. MIGA employed an external consultant to conduct a confidential and anonymous survey of all of its clients and to compare the results with a previous survey conducted in 1994. The Client Satisfaction Survey had a high rate of return (73 percent). The results were gratifying for the Agency. For example, most of the investors (94 percent) reported that they would return to MIGA if they sought political risk insurance in the future and would recommend MIGA to others (see Box 1). The survey also verified how critical are MIGA's services for facilitating investment in our developing member countries. MIGA clients were directly asked: *"With regard to your last contract of guarantee, how important was it for your firm to secure a MIGA guarantee before proceeding with the investment?"* Most of the surveyed investors (77 percent) considered the investment insurance coverage they have procured from MIGA as critical in proceeding with their planned investment. This Satisfaction Survey also elicited some useful suggestions and criticisms that have formed a basis for future program improvements.

Box 1. Quality of MIGA's Services

In an effort to gauge investors' perceptions of MIGA's service quality and their inclination to use MIGA insurance again, MIGA incorporated a specific question in the survey of its clients; they were directly asked:
"If you needed political risk insurance in the future, would you purchase from MIGA again?"

	Yes:	No:	No answer:
	94%	0%	6%

To measure investors' inclinations to recommend MIGA to others, they were asked:
"Would you recommend MIGA Guarantee Services to other corporations which inquire about your experience with MIGA?"

	Yes:	No:	No answer:
	94%	0%	6%

Phase II of this effort, *Project Monitoring Design and Testing*, was completed in 1997. There were three tasks associated with Phase II. First, a Project Monitoring Questionnaire was designed to elicit information concerning the project's *actual* developmental effect in the host country; detailed instructions for its completion by investors were prepared; and staff who would be undertaking the monitoring tasks were trained. Second, this phase was intended to supply some preliminary information with respect to the *actual* developmental impact of a small sample of investments. Finally, MIGA viewed this phase as an opportunity to test and revise, if necessary, the system and the questionnaire to make it both respond to MIGA's needs and to make it as user-friendly as possible. It was recognized early in this evaluation process that this would be an evolutionary process for MIGA. A program of project site visits was initiated, and as the number of evaluated projects increased, MIGA had an opportunity to test, revise, and improve the evaluation system and the questionnaire to make them more relevant to MIGA's information needs. MIGA implemented "real-time" improvements (i.e., as soon as shortcomings and solutions were identified).

MIGA intends to continue to improve its comprehensive evaluation efforts in the next few years. In addition, MIGA has already began undertaking the in-depth studies planned for a later phase of this program (those are included in Section IV).

B. Selection of Projects for Evaluation

Selection of projects to be evaluated followed a simple and straightforward initial rule: a contract of guarantee should be active and "mature," in other words, the project should have been in operation for a period of time sufficient to produce reasonably reliable results.[2] Normally, a project should be operational for five years (but not less than three years) before monitoring. MIGA took into consideration that certain projects require more time to mature, thus choosing to defer the candidacy of some active contracts for a later round of monitoring when their full effects can be more fairly appraised.

The time needed for a project to mature varies across sectors. Projects in the infrastructure, manufacturing, and, especially, the mining sectors generally have longer completion cycles, and thus their respective contracts are usually not mature for monitoring before the fourth year.[3] On the other hand, projects in tourism and those considered as "Other Services" (e.g., distributors/retailers) require fewer years to demonstrate meaningful results for evaluation purposes. Regarding financial sector investments, projects involving branch banks might be ready for evaluation as early as the third year. Financial subsidiaries and affiliates (e.g., mortgage lending, leasing, pension funds) need additional time for their financial products to penetrate the market and thus require a longer period to mature.

However, contracts to be evaluated were not chosen solely based on the number of years the project has been fully operational. Other considerations were also taken into account, such as cost efficiency, project representativeness, and the sample's regional and sectoral diversification.

C. Selection of Monitoring Officers

The evaluation program was designed to be both impartial and highly participatory in nature. It was envisaged that it would draw upon the Agency's internal staff and, where

---

[2] Several contracts may correspond to one project, given the participation of more than one investor and the existence of more than one type of investment (e.g., debt, equity, etc.) that requires individual contractual coverage.

[3] All mining sector projects in the population of "mature" contracts were guaranteed in 1995 or subsequently, and thus MIGA has opted to postpone their evaluation until the next monitoring round, when they will be operational for at least four years.

appropriate and cost effective, the assistance of outside consultants. The selective use of consultant assistance was to assure a degree of impartiality yet not constitute an undue financial drain. To further conserve limited Agency resources, MIGA also proposed to solicit the assistance of clients to carry out a process of simplified self-evaluation.

MIGA believes that there are important benefits from assigning staff members who were not directly involved in the original project underwriting process participate in the evaluation process. It especially boosts morale when the staff are able to confirm the beneficial developmental effects of the MIGA-supported projects on the host countries. Even in instances where projects have not performed as anticipated, the staff better understands the problems encountered and can avoid them in the future. In this way, MIGA believes that the system will be effective only if it has been thoroughly internalized by Agency personnel. Their participation in the program has and will strengthen their analysis of developmental impacts to be used in their future underwriting.

On the other hand, the selective use of outside expertise in the project evaluation process is equally important because scrutiny by disinterested parties brings a fresh perspective and ensures the credibility of the evaluation program. The external evaluator employed in this monitoring round has also made valuable suggestions on how to revise the evaluation system based on feedback from both investors and monitoring officers.

In the first monitoring round, 56 percent of the 25 evaluations were performed by nine MIGA staff members. One project was evaluated "by mail" (see Project Evaluation Process), and the remaining 10 projects were evaluated by an independent consultant.

In order to conserve resources, consultant trips were always designed to evaluate multiple MIGA-assisted projects in the host country. When possible, projects in neighboring countries were also monitored during the course of one trip.

D. Evaluation Sample

MIGA evaluated 25 projects during the first monitoring round, corresponding to 39 contracts of guarantee. This sample of contracts monitored represents 44 percent of the number of active contracts issued between fiscal years 1990–1995 (Table 2).[4] Table 2 demonstrates the effort to monitor as many of MIGA's older contracts as possible, since they can provide more measurable impacts than more recent contracts.

The 25 evaluated projects are sectorally and regionally diversified. These projects are located in 13 countries: Argentina, Bangladesh, Brazil, Costa Rica, China, Indonesia, Kazakhstan, Pakistan, Peru, Saudi Arabia, South Africa, Trinidad and Tobago, and Turkey. The projects include investments in metal forging, the production of

---

[4] MIGA has been able to monitor two contracts issued in fiscal 1996 and three canceled contracts (corresponding to four projects in all). These contracts are not included in the comparison performed in Figures 4 and 5, since they are not part of the population. (The convenience of scheduled business trips influenced the selection of these contracts.) The issue of evaluating terminated contracts remains under review by the Agency given the difficulties of obtaining adequate data in a timely manner.

Table 2. Guarantee Contracts Evaluated
        (as of June 1998)

	FY90	FY91*	FY92	FY93	FY94	FY95	Total†
Active guarantee contracts	0	5	7	7	19	39	77
Active contracts evaluated‡	0	2	6	7	11	8	34 **(44%)**
Canceled contracts evaluated		1			2		3

* Three contracts related to one project are not yet operational; however, the investor expects the project to go forward.
† In addition, two contracts issued in fiscal 1996 also were monitored.
‡ Active as of December 30, 1997.

fertilizers, glass, pharmaceuticals, trucks/buses, garments, and the processing of steel slag. There is one project each in ecotourism, telecommunications, and airline catering services. The sample also includes 10 banking projects, a mortgage and a leasing program, and two pension funds (see the Annex for a complete listing).

Below in Figures 4 and 5 are the disaggregated data on active contracts monitored by region and sector, comparing them with the universe of mature contracts. (The number of active guarantee contracts issued during fiscal years 90–95 constitutes the universe or population of mature contracts.) Note that since contracts related to financial projects mature earlier than those in other sectors, they make up a higher percentage of contracts evaluated. Although the sample is reasonably representative of the universe of mature contracts, its size (34 contracts) remains small *vis-à-vis* MIGA's total active portfolio (227 contracts as of June 30, 1998).

Figure 4. Active vs. Evaluated Contracts by Region, Fiscal Years 1990–95

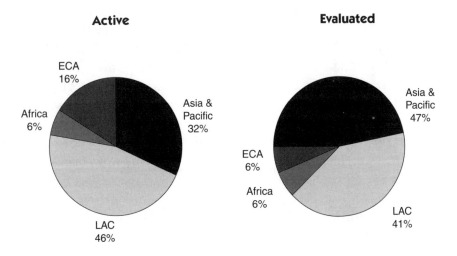

Figure 5. Active vs. Evaluated Contracts by Industry, Fiscal Years 1990–95

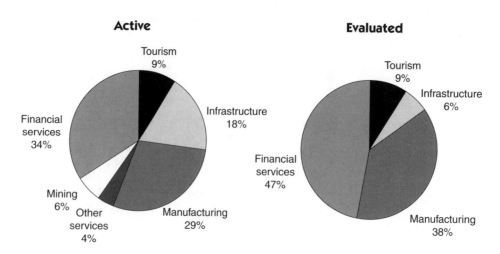

E. Project Evaluation Process

The project evaluation process is intended to elicit information on the *actual* developmental impacts of the projects on the host country. This information allows MIGA to compare *a priori* estimates provided by the investors at the time of application for a MIGA guarantee with *ex-post facto* results. In order to maximize efficiency and to minimize the burden on MIGA's clients, the Project Monitoring Questionnaire presented to investors essentially mirrors the confidential information requested in the Definitive Application on a wide range of developmental information.

As part of the preparatory work for the monitoring trip, monitoring officers are thoroughly briefed on project-specific developmental issues so that, for consistency purposes, they will retrieve data following a standard set of development variables—introduced and discussed in subsequent sections (see Section III). During the trip, the monitoring officer visits the project site, meets with investors to discuss the answers to the Project Monitoring Questionnaire and collect additional data; when merited, other concerned parties are interviewed. In addition, staff often consulted with IBRD/IFC officials on issues regarding host country programs and strategies. The information included in the project evaluation report is entered and analyzed; the results are disseminated to MIGA Management and staff, the Board of Directors, and the general public through publications.[5] The flowchart below (Figure 6) traces this process.

The project evaluation process is intended to be a cooperative effort between the investor and MIGA. Investors are responsible for filling out the Project Monitoring Questionnaire, meeting the visiting MIGA monitoring officer, and supplying additional information as needed. (If necessary, evaluation staff contact the investor after the visit to request additional data.) The investor's degree of involvement and coop-

---

[5] MIGA requests written consent from the investor before disclosing any sensitive project-specific information to the general public.

Figure 6. Project Evaluation Process

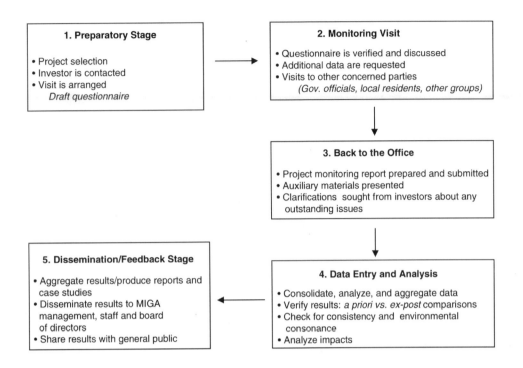

eration largely determines the success of the monitoring visit and the quality of information gathered. The investor is assured in writing that MIGA will keep the results of the project-specific monitoring process confidential unless specific investor consent is obtained. In general, MIGA received outstanding cooperation from investors.

In one case, MIGA tried a new approach of sending a questionnaire by mail, without the benefit of a site visit. Cooperation of the investor in this single instance was outstanding and the evaluation report submitted was rich in information. The investor's report commented on MIGA's role, volunteered an assessment of the investor's other MIGA-related projects, and provided a detailed analysis of the role of foreign banks in developing countries. However, it is uncertain if this approach will work as successfully with all investors. While this mail-in approach enables MIGA to assess more projects and conserve resources, the approach precludes complete verification of the information submitted.

III. Results on the Ground

A. Introduction

MIGA's first monitoring round encompassed the evaluation of 25 projects. While all projects were found to have generated some positive developmental impacts, the degree and nature of such impacts varied greatly from project to project; they include such impacts as the transfer of knowledge, contribution to social development and poverty alleviation, support to the development of the financial sector and capital markets, creation of indirect jobs, and benefits to businesses related to the project. These effects are described following a multidimensional approach to development introduced later in this paper.

A project also has a direct effect on the host country's economy. However, the overall impact of a single private sector project on the national economy, or its relation to a sector is, almost always small. Analytically, this precludes MIGA from meaningfully utilizing standard macroeconomic measures of development such as GNP per capita growth, export growth, fiscal sustainability, and the sectoral contribution made by the project. Nonetheless, the next section reports on the aggregate results of this evaluation with respect to those economic indicators that could be measured across all projects.

B. Verification of Direct Economic Effects

The initial intent of MIGA's evaluation process is to *verify* the extent to which the applicant's anticipated developmental impacts are realized, once the project was fully operational. (This verification is possible due to the systematic gathering of *a priori* data from the applicant. Given the conceptual and practical difficulties of building counterfactual scenarios, this *a priori* data provides valuable baseline information). Some developmental measures cut across sectors, and their aggregation is both possible and meaningful in giving an indication of the overall developmental impact of projects; other impacts are not so easily measured and aggregated.[6] Hence, it is useful to start by reporting the results of selected indicators that can be utilized across all projects. In an effort to finding common and comparable units of measurement, four such indicators were selected: taxes/duties paid, exports generated,[7] number of new jobs directly created, and total investment facilitated (Table 3). However, MIGA wants to emphasize that these four indicators are not the only ones of interest to the Agency.

---

[6] In addition to the verification of estimated impacts, aggregate numbers (as those presented in Table 3) are also useful to assess the size of the impact.

[7] Although MIGA attempts to measure the net impact on the host country's balance of payments, it was not meaningful to aggregate the retrieved data since (1) there was no case in which the investors was able to calculate the import substitution effect; and (2) in most cases, export-generating companies in the sample do not pay dividends (capital outflow) until the fourth or fifth year of operation.

Table 3. Selected Developmental Impacts, 25 Evaluated Projects
(US$ millions, unless stated otherwise)

	Anticipated	Actual	Percent Difference
Annual taxes and duties paid to the government	53.5	87.4	+63
Annual exports generated*	353.1	399.8	+13
Number of new jobs directly created	5,026	5,796†	+15
Total project investment facilitated	1,358.3	1,546.4	+14

* Includes only the eight export-generating projects.

† Includes one project that had expatriate labor from other developing countries.

As Table 3 shows, on aggregate, the investments' impacts were greater than anticipated at the time of the underwriting. Actual total investment was 14 percent higher than anticipated (about US$1.5 billion), reflecting additional inflows of funds. Taxes paid to the host governments were 63 percent higher than anticipated, and exports generated were also higher than anticipated (13 percent). MIGA's leverage effect has also been quite significant. The 25 projects that MIGA monitored during the first round have facilitated about US$1.5 billion in total project investment to 13 developing countries. This amount is three times the amount of coverage that MIGA issued to these guarantee holders.

Thus, in broad terms, the initial estimates supplied by the investors have been conservative forecasts of the actual impacts. This is particularly noteworthy if we take into consideration that the anticipated data were gathered on the basis of five-year forecasts, and many of these projects have not been in operation for that period of time. Indeed, the average "age" of the 25 evaluated projects is four years. It is expected that the impacts will be greater once the five-year operational period for each project is reached.

But despite the tax revenues, exports generated, new jobs created, and the amount of investment facilitated, MIGA recognizes that the size of the projects are relatively small compared to the economies of most host countries.[8] Of the 25 projects monitored, 13 had a minimal impact on their respective countries' economies (see Table 5 at the end of this section). These 13 projects were found to be small either relative to the overall economy or to the particular sector.

Two projects were considered to have an outstanding impact on the host countries' economies. KAFCO in Bangladesh and PCS Nitrogen-Arcadian in Trinidad and Tobago have generated significant export and tax revenues for their respective host governments. In addition, these projects significantly supported their govern-

---

[8] As opposed to public sector investment and projects funded by the IBRD, which are designed to target specific economic sectors, Foreign Direct Investment tends to have a relatively smaller influence on the economy of the host country.

ments' economic reform programs. Arcadian Partners, L.P.s participated in the first major privatization sale in Trinidad and Tobago, while KAFCO was the first private joint-venture fertilizer company in Bangladesh.

C. Types of Developmental Impacts, Conceptual Framework, and Evaluation Findings

1. A Typology of Developmental Effects

For analytical purposes, MIGA has adopted a multidimensional approach to development by distinguishing between three types of developmental effects: direct effects, indirect effects, and diffused effects (see Figure 7). This typology, utilized to structure the next section of this report, distinguishes the degree to which developmental effects can be identified and measured. Direct effects usually can be systematically measured in terms of, for example, the project's investment in human capital, its creation of employment, its contribution to government tax revenues, and exports generated (direct economic effects). As expected, the causal nature of the connection between the investment and these effects is usually clear and direct.

Figure 7. Types of Developmental Impacts

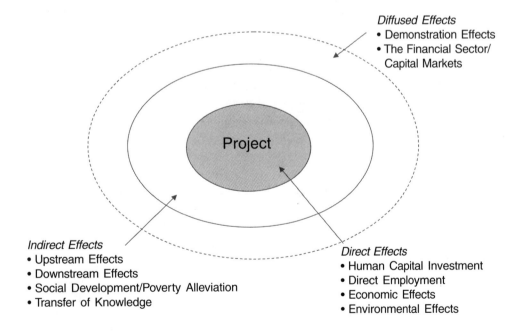

On the other hand, indirect effects usually are by-products of the project's business activities, and the causal connection to the investment is more difficult to measure. Such effects include upstream and downstream effects (which include indirect employment generation), social development and poverty alleviation, and the transfer of knowledge. Diffused effects include impacts on the financial sector and capital markets, and demonstration effects. These and other developmental impacts can influence many socioeconomic entities before diffusing into a host country's economy as a whole; they are very difficult to measure. (Table 5 gives a summary of these impacts in MIGA's 25 evaluated projects.)

2. Direct Effects

Human Capital Investment

Economists have recognized that the knowledge possessed by human beings forms the basis for achieving increases in total factor productivity. While land, labor, and physical capital are subject to diminishing returns, human knowledge is not. Moreover, knowledge's distinguishing characteristic is that the use of it by one individual does not diminish its availability to others.

For many developing nations, the slow growth of knowledge constitutes a severe constraint on the process of modernization. One of the most direct ways to accelerate development is through investment in human resources. Thus, expenditures on skills training and education, health and nutrition, and research and development all contribute to productivity by improving the quality of the country's population. Human capital improvement has been traditionally measured by the average number of years of formal education in the population—a measure that ignores other forms of education. Specifically, a powerful development argument for job training rests on the recognition that it takes a considerable amount of time and money to raise the knowledge of workers in developing countries through the formal educational system. In the meantime, on-the-job training offers a more direct and cost-efficient way of fulfilling skilled manpower needs.

All evaluated projects implemented general training for their employees. However, MIGA also tried to measure the additional specialized training made available to employees as a result of the project's implementation.[9] It was gratifying to verify that about half of the evaluated projects provided specific "value-added" training (see Table 4).

Table 4. Type of Training Provided by MIGA-Assisted Projects

Sector	Total projects	General training	Specialized project training
Financial Services	14	14	4
Manufacturing	7	7	6
Other Services	4	4	4
Total	25	25	14

---

[9] MIGA has not assessed the benefits of general training versus specific training. Specialized training in the context of this analysis refers to training programs, alongside general training, available *exclusively* to employees involved in the project enterprise.

In addition, MIGA tried to measure access to training by both existing and new employees, the range of courses offered, the average number of staff hours devoted to training, and any evidence of productivity increases as a result of the training program offered. MIGA also considered the implementation of Technical Agreements and Total Quality Management (TQM) programs as evidence of the investor's commitment to improve the enterprise's human capital base. It was equally gratifying to find that 11 out of 14 projects that offered "specialized" training had outstanding training programs (see Table 5). These programs were provided in a wide variety of investments—"greenfield" projects, joint-ventures, financial projects that initiated full-scale operations, and projects that support financial subsidiaries and affiliates.

In some financial sector projects (e.g., expanding branch bank operations), MIGA was not able to retrieve more detailed information regarding their investment in human capital. In general, their contribution to the enhancement of human capacity is positive. These institutions provide extensive training in banking and finance to employees at the managerial/professional level, and basic training to those involved in bank operations. ING Bank, Citibank N.A., Crédit Agricole Indosuez, Société Générale, and other global finance groups provide training at their head offices for employees in their branches located worldwide.

Box 2. Investment in Human Capital: SAS Partners/ Gate Gourmet, Turkey

In fiscal 1990, MIGA issued a guarantee to cover SAS Service Partner's (SSP) equity interest in Usas Uçak Servisi Anonim Sirketi (USAS). USAS was a state-owned enterprise that provided airline catering and restaurant services throughout Turkey. In 1994, Scandinavian Airline System (SAS) sold SSP to Gate Gourmet Holdings, Ltd.

The investors designed a Technical Support Agreement that specified the transfer of a range of technical and managerial skills, including Total Quality Management (TQM) training, to local employees within a five-year period. The agreement, set at 21,000 man-hours annually, transferred the technical know-how accumulated by SPP over the last 20 years. Overall productivity for 1995 and 1996 increased by 6 percent for each of these years.

In 1996 alone, the Airline Catering division increased its production efficiency per man-hour by 9 percent; while the Airport Restaurants division increased its sales by 99 percent and improved its efficiency (in terms of items sold per man-hour) by 4 percent. USAS Turkey has also reversed its reputation from being a low to a high quality service provider; it currently serves over 50 airlines—including British Airways, Singapore Airlines, Delta Airlines, Cathay Pacific, and Air France—compared to only one airline customer in 1989. The company has since reaped rewards for its TQM training program by earning the internationally prestigious ISO 9001 certification.

Examples:

Komatsu–Indonesia: As stipulated in the project's License and Technical Agreement, a significant percentage of this metal forging plant's labor force undergoes training in forging technology and quality inspection each year. In addition, one worker is selected yearly, based on performance, to receive additional year-long training in Japan. The company also has enlisted the Astra Management Development Institute (AMDI), a training arm of a prominent Indonesian conglomerate, to provide management skills training. At a more general level, each new worker receives a week of safety rules orientation prior to commencing work.

ABN–AMRO Bank–Kazakhstan: Employees (numbering about 100) at this newly established bank branch undertook training programs in credit analysis, international accounting, treasury operation, and commercial negotiations. Many of the local employees were also sent overseas within ABN AMRO's international network. On-the-job training included such things as working with technology-intensive equipment and acquiring basic English language skills.

AFP Integra–Peru: This private pension fund manager provides extensive training programs for its employees given the pioneering nature of this business in the country.

Direct Employment

There is a virtual consensus among economists and policy makers that, in most countries, unemployment and underemployment remain key obstacles to achieving economic development. In MIGA's evaluation system, direct employment is defined as the number of employees, excluding expatriates,[10] that a company hires specifically because of the investment. The actual experience, verified by the monitoring and evaluation process, is very favorable in terms of jobs created. On an aggregate basis, these 25 evaluated projects have created 5,796 jobs, or 15 percent more than anticipated at the time of underwriting (see Table 3).

Figure 8 below notes the creation of jobs, by sector, of these 25 projects. The 4,608 new jobs directly created in only seven manufacturing projects is noteworthy. Although the actual number of jobs directly created by financial projects is more than three times what was originally anticipated, this is largely due to the creation of jobs by financial subsidiaries and affiliates, like mortgage or pension fund management companies.

---

[10] In one project, expatriates were counted because they are unskilled immigrants from several developing countries and represented the majority of the workforce.

Figure 8. Number of New Jobs Created, 25 Evaluated Projects

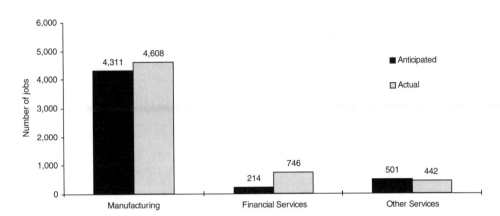

In industrial sector projects, the direct employment effect is often relatively clear-cut since most of them entail a green field operation (i.e., the construction and operation of a new enterprise). Thus, the direct employment effect in such projects as KAFCO-Bangladesh (more than 600 jobs created) or Crescent Greenwood Pakistan (about 2,663 individuals employed) has been outstanding. Relatively smaller projects, such as Suzhou-Lederle Pharmaceutical in China and Guardian Glass in Saudi Arabia, created fewer jobs, but their contribution to reduce unemployment rates remains positive.[11]

There are some problems related to the accurate measurement of direct employment effects. For example, MIGA's guarantee allowed Volvo Perú to offer better financing terms to customers, thus contributing to increased sales of trucks and buses. Conceivably, the increase in demand compelled the company to hire at least some new workers to meet this demand. It was verified that the company had a considerable increase in employment levels since MIGA issued the guarantee. The investor, however, could not accurately differentiate these workers hired as a result of the MIGA guarantee versus those hired for other reasons. Despite these considerations, the project had contributed positively to employment generation. Another measurement problem is the loss of jobs due to restructuring and/or privatization. Follow-up investments could create some new jobs in related projects. The net employment effect, however, would be difficult to quantify.

MIGA faces a severe measurement dilemma with respect to financial projects that are expanding branch bank operations. Usually, MIGA does not attribute any direct employment creation to these financial projects, since the changes in employment levels observed cannot be attributed solely to the MIGA guarantee; they might be due to other factors related to the dynamics of business growth. To be conservative, therefore, MIGA does not claim any direct employment effect of such projects as ING Bank and BankBoston in Brazil, Crédit Agricole Indosuez in Pakistan, and Citibank N.A. in Argentina.

---

[11] Within the partial equilibrium analytical framework used in this paper, it is appropriate to conclude that the creation of new sources of employment has a positive net impact on unemployment levels prevailing in the host country.

In the case of banks that initiate new operations in a given country, this employment effect can be important and relatively easy to measure. ABN AMRO, for example, hired more than 100 local employees in Kazakhstan. However, even in such cases, measuring the direct employment effect is not always clear-cut. For example, MIGA supported Société Générale's initial operations in Pakistan and counted their impacts. Later, the bank opened two more branches in Lahore and Islamabad. Should employees hired for these new branches be in some way attributable to the investment guaranteed by MIGA?

Financial sector investments in subsidiaries and affiliates such as mortgage or leasing programs generally entail the creation of a new office or division and thus the company hires a specific number of employees. For example, Banco de Boston in Argentina employed 200 new staff in its new mortgage program (see case study in Section IV).[12] Although the number of new jobs is typically smaller than those in manufacturing projects, the employment effect is nevertheless considered outstanding in countries where the financial sector itself is not a significant source of employment.

The Environment

The process of evaluating developmental impacts included careful attention to environmental matters and safety concerns. The Agency is cognizant of the importance of environmental soundness and sustainability in the development process. Therefore, MIGA's evaluation of developmental effectiveness included environmental as well as economic matters. During the monitoring trip, the monitoring officer was asked to undertake a reconnaissance of the project site, reporting general environmental observations and any unusual conditions to MIGA's environmental expert, who then assessed the need for further action.

MIGA is satisfied with the environmental impacts of the monitored projects.[13] In some cases, the environmental aspect was exemplary; in a few others, MIGA noted potential problems. In those few cases where potential concerns were observed, MIGA followed up promptly with discussions with the investors. As a result, MIGA was able to satisfactorily resolve its concerns promptly.

This form of monitoring has proved to be useful because on-site observations give MIGA greater confidence that sound environmental standards are being adhered to. The type of observations made by monitoring officers are exemplified below.

Sometimes projects exceed World Bank Guidelines by, for example, implementing innovative environmental programs and/or undergoing periodic third-party environmental assessments. Crescent Greenwood in Pakistan had an outstanding environmental program (see case study in Section IV). The evaluation process also

---

[12] However, in some cases, financial institutions could decide to reassign existing personnel to assume additional duties. This is taken into consideration when trying to measure the employment effect as accurately as possible.

[13] In the case of Motorola in Pakistan and all 14 evaluated financial sector investments, environmental effects were not assessed.

> *Examples:*
>
> **American Home Product—China:** The only by-product of the Suzhou Lederle Pharmaceutical Company's production plant is treated process water. The water being discharged into the adjacent canal was in fact significantly cleaner than the water being taken from it. (In 1995, an environmental inspection conducted by two independent auditors reported very favorable results as well.)
>
> **Komatsu—Indonesia:** Safety is emphasized with the display of large signs. Workers wear proper safety attire, including hard hats, ear plugs, hard protective shoes, and face guards as appropriate to their work station; management trains all newly recruited staff on worker safety. An expert from the Astra Group reports on the company's environmental conditions every six months. MIGA's representative checked the procedure for waste water treatment and the disposal of scrap metal, and provided the collected information for further review by MIGA's environmental advisor.

encountered a few instances in which investors' environmental practices raised concerns. MIGA found investors' cooperation was a key to resolving these concerns. The case depicted below highlights the importance of site visits and exemplifies the shared interest between MIGA and the investor in mitigating environmental risks; it does not represent an example of adverse environmental impacts.[14]

> *Example:*
>
> **KAFCO—Bangladesh:** During the course of the evaluation, the investor supplied MIGA with an agreed Hazard Operations Analysis, undertaken in December 1994, and a Study Supplement of March 1995. The IFC assisted MIGA by reviewing these analyses for consonance with World Bank Guidelines. The IFC found that the Hazard Operations Analysis was, in general terms, "following acceptable principles for preparation of a hazard assessment." At the same time, however, the IFC raised some questions on the assumptions utilized and suggested that an important modification in the approach to the Hazard Operations Analysis be undertaken. KAFCO welcomed this recommendation, and, in response to MIGA's suggestion, the project enterprise prepared a new Hazard Operations Analysis, and submitted it to MIGA in April, 1997. This new study takes into consideration the suggestions made by the IFC for new modeling (and a set of consequence calculations) for a large accidental leakage from the plant. It was reviewed by the IFC Environmental Division and found to be of high quality and demonstrated "good professionalism." The project enterprise found the results to be very useful and made several changes in its emergency response systems.

---

[14] In fact, the investor's response was exemplary. The investor was under no obligation to follow the IFC's suggestion, since the initial Hazard Operations Analysis was in compliance with World Bank Guidelines.

Box 3. Environmental Effect: The Rain Forest Aerial Tram, Costa Rica

In fiscal 1995, MIGA supported the construction and operation of a 1.3 km aerial tram, a restaurant, and a visitor/research center located on a 338 hectares site bordering Braulio Carrillo National Park in Costa Rica (50 km north of San José). MIGA issued guarantee contracts covering foreign investment in Dosel S.A., a special purpose company set to run the Rain Forest Aerial Tram (RFAT). One contract guarantees the equity invested by Conservation Tourism, Ltd., of the United States against currency transfer risk; the other guarantee contract covers Bank of Nova Scotia's (Canada) nonshareholder loan to Dosel against Transfer Restriction, Expropriation, and War and Civil Disturbance.

The project is structured to make a sensitive economic use of Costa Rica's rain forest, preserving and protecting it by utilizing the environment in a nonintrusive way. Furthermore, Dosel hopes to work closely with the government to reduce illegal hunting activities. Because of its commitment to the environment, the project has been named a "National Resource" by the President of Costa Rica.

In addition to making significant efforts to ensure minimal adverse impact on the environment, the company allocates resources for research and educational purposes. As of 1998, the RFAT plans to construct lodging facilities to accommodate visiting research scientists. High safety and waste-treatment standards are in place. Furthermore, the project sponsors an environmental education program to improve environmental awareness about the importance of protecting the rain forests. Within this program, admission for Costa Rican school children and students is free or reduced; 3,000 children/students participated in 1996 (an estimated 9,000 will participate in 1998).

3. Indirect Effects

Upstream and Downstream Effects

Economists often use the concept of linkages when they describe inducement mechanisms within production processes and subsequent cumulative effects. More specifically, backward linkages refer to how the addition of new enterprises create a derived demand for inputs, benefiting those companies that supply them. On the other hand, forward linkages involve how the establishment of a company might stimulate other industries that use the new output as input in their production cycle. MIGA evaluation staff have used this terminology in the past, but will utilize the concept of backward and forward linkages in a modified fashion in this report to identify the ways in which a project can help stimulate economic gains for related businesses, and, indirectly, create new jobs. Upstream effects (backward linkages) describe how a new or expanding company benefits their suppliers of goods and services. Downstream effects (forward linkages) illustrate how this company's clients—unrelated to the project—gain from an increase in business. In turn, benefits stemming from these two effects generally translate into higher overall employment levels.

– 24 –

Upstream Effects in Manufacturing, Infrastructure, and Service Projects

Generally, monitoring reveals that most manufacturing projects share the same type of upstream effects. These projects often have a high percentage of local procurement for goods and services, and their business enhances economic activities in the area. The strength of upstream effects depends on such factors as the project size, the level of local procurement, and the number of suppliers benefited. KAFCO-Bangladesh and PCS Nitrogen-Arcadian in Trinidad and Tobago are examples of outstanding projects in this regard. It has been observed that upstream effects are positive in many other manufacturing projects, for they often involve construction contracts and local procurement of fuel and oil, spare parts, repair and maintenance services, transportation, catering, and janitorial services.

Examples:

Volvo Perú: The expansion of customer financing operations for this local manufacturer of buses and trucks caused its sales to grow, stimulating it to increase local sourcing considerably. Although it is difficult to estimate the subsequent indirect employment creation, it would be safe to assume that the increase in business activity was substantial. (In 1995, a high percentage of the parts used in the production process were manufactured by the company's local suppliers, which employ about 7,000 employees.)

SAS Partners/Gate Gourmet—Turkey: The investor's participation in the privatization of the Turkish state-owned airline catering and airport restaurant enterprise helped to turn the company into a profitable operation. The company purchases almost all its food and other supplies from local companies.

Upstream effects are not evident in every project. Some projects import almost all their raw materials from their parent company. In the case of Komatsu in Indonesia, for example, key raw materials that met specifications could not be procured locally, and thus the company had to import them. In Pakistan, Motorola currently has to import cellular phones and other technical equipment.

Downstream Effects in Manufacturing, Infrastructure, and Service Projects

The monitoring revealed a wide range of downstream effects. These included improvements in infrastructure such as housing and road construction, installation of telecommunications, and electricity. Some projects outsourced distribution services. One project is using a local trucking company for the delivery of spare parts and tools used in production, as well as for delivering its products. The construction of a large manufacturing plant benefits local real estate offices, medical centers, and schools in the surrounding community. In the Costa Rican ecotourism project, downstream effects include the influence of tourism on hotel accommodations, gift shops, and restaurants. Suzhou-Lederle in China supplies local pharmaceutical distributors, who then resell the product to hospitals and drug stores.

Volvo Perú's downstream effects are outstanding. Their output (trucks and buses) are inputs for microentrepreneurs and small firms that offer transportation services in the country. The company estimated that MIGA's guaranteed funds supported the financed sale of 400 trucks and buses. In addition to the establishment of new businesses and/or the expansion of existing operations, two drivers and two assistants are needed to operate each unit and handle the cargo. Therefore, a potential 1,600 new jobs have been indirectly created and other businesses have sprung as a result of this operation.

Two projects demonstrated minimal downstream effects for the host country. One project's entire production is exported to the parent company. Nevertheless, even in this case (Komatsu in Indonesia), 90 percent of this project's employees rent housing around the project site, contributing to increased income levels in the local community. In the case of the other project (MultiServ in South Africa), downstream effects are limited due to the project's particular business activity; it recovers stainless steel for a client from their remnant slags.

Upstream and Downstream Effects in Financial Sector Projects

A financial institution can direct loans towards multiple "subprojects" that produce further downstream and upstream effects in an exponential-like mode. The nature of these effects in the financial sector differ in many aspects from those in other sectors and therefore require a separate discussion. These effects have developmental impacts that are difficult to measure.

In general, financial sector projects do not have a strong direct employment effect relative to other sectors (e.g., manufacturing and services), but they tend to create more employment indirectly. Direct employment generated by "subprojects" is the most significant component of the financial institution's indirect job creation.

Because of insufficient information, MIGA is unable to trace and usually does not seek to measure downstream effects of a MIGA guarantee in an already operating branch bank (e.g., Bank of America, Crédit Agricole Indosuez in Pakistan) or financial institution (e.g., the two private pension funds in Peru) due to complex methodological issues. However, when the guaranteed funds are earmarked for a specific use, the "subprojects" are easier to identify. Beneficial effects can then be traced.

> ### Examples:
>
> **ING Bank–Brazil:** The bank branch disbursed loans to support, among others, the largest leasing institution and the second largest retail bank in Brazil, a local truck dealer, and a gas bottler.
>
> **Citibank N.A.–Argentina:** This financial institution facilitated investments of more than US$100 million in Argentina by financing the digitalization of telecommunication lines, the construction of a new gas treatment plant, the extension of gas pipelines, the purchase and installation of the new subway signaling system, and by providing working capital to a steel company and two hydroelectric plants.

On the other hand, projects that support the development of a specific financial product (i.e., financial subsidiaries and affiliates) have identifiable downstream effects, most of which are outstanding.

> ### Examples:
>
> **AFP Integra—Perú:** The portfolio of AFP Integra, invested domestically in non-financial companies, was about US$260 million as of June 1998. (These funds purchased common stock and corporate bonds.) Approximately US$160 million was invested in 23 companies in the food and drink, metals, cement, machinery and equipment, fishing, real state, and mining industries; US$100 million was invested in five companies in the utilities sector (e.g., energy, telecommunications). In addition, AFP Integra purchased shares (worth a total of US$30 million) from 2 financial companies. Previously, all of the companies that AFP Integra invested in had limited or no access to the local capital market to raise funds. The growth and sophistication of the pension system also stimulated the demand for labor in the financial sector (e.g., traders, financial analysts, accountants, etc.).
>
> **BankBoston, Leasing—Brazil:** The leasing company increased its loan portfolio with medium-term dollar-denominated loans given to small and medium-size companies. This in itself represents a downstream effect; however, a more distinct effect can be traced to the increase in business for local companies that sell the capital equipment leased in this program (100 percent of the purchased equipment is procured locally).

In sum, the form and strength of downstream effects are specific to each project. It is often observed that these types of effects are present in the manufacturing sector more often than in the financial sector. Nonetheless, although manufacturing projects demonstrate more "tangible" downstream effects, financial institutions often have downstream effects that are far greater in scope. However, MIGA found downstream effects associated with the expansion of branch bank operations to be more difficult to trace given the fungible nature of money. Attempting to do so would require an extensive analysis of an institution's loan portfolio. A more quantitative measurement would entail a "second-level" investigation involving the business activities of each bank client.

The same constraint affects the measurement of upstream effects. In projects that support the expansion of branch bank operations, guaranteed funds help increase a branch bank's loan portfolio, expand its services, and thus its client base. Higher transaction volumes require an increase in the supply of operating materials and equipment to sustain the increase in operations. Undeniably, upstream effects are also present in financial projects. However, these effects are relatively small given the financial sector's low procurement needs compared to the manufacturing sector. As with downstream effects, they are difficult to trace; other variables cannot be controlled to measure the upstream effect attributable to the project's implementation.

However, upstream effects related to projects that support the initiation of full-scale commercial banking activities are stronger and more easily identified, since these projects constitute new business for local suppliers. (ABN-AMRO in Kazakhstan and Société Générale in Pakistan, for example, built new relationships with local suppliers.)

Social Development and Poverty Alleviation

Alleviating poverty is the primary goal of development. Towards that end, the World Bank Group aims to reduce poverty through an overall strategy of inclusive development that involves partnerships among the Bank Group entities, other development institutions, the government involved, program beneficiaries, and the private sector. MIGA, dealing solely with private sector investors as its vehicle, rarely has an opportunity to directly reduce poverty. Such investors, in search of customers of their own goods and services, do not often locate their investments in the most needy countries or serve the needs of the poorest of the poor. Nevertheless, MIGA seeks to measure to what extent these private enterprises have, directly or indirectly, contributed to the overall social development and to poverty alleviation in their host countries.

In its eight years of guarantee operations, MIGA has facilitated US$25 billion of investments to 62 developing countries, of which 26 are IDA-eligible countries. Although it is difficult to verify the degree of overall poverty alleviation, at the project level MIGA's support has contributed to increased employment opportunities (especially for women) and workers' welfare, and provided much-needed social infrastructure that host governments are unable to undertake.

Of the 25 projects monitored in the first round, eight projects are in IDA-eligible countries. These projects in IDA countries employ a total of 4,323 workers, of whom 1,644 are unskilled. Monitoring results also show that six projects have had clearly measurable social developmental impacts to their host economies (see Table 5). All of these projects tended to pay more than their host country's minimum wage and more than that of other foreign joint ventures. Higher wages not only serve to attract high-quality staff but also translate into higher incomes for the staff and their families. For example, in 1997, Crescent Greenwood's unskilled workforce in Pakistan earned an average of US$750 annually, in a country where the current minimum wage was set at US$585 annually, and where the per capita GDP was US$460. Seamstresses in this factory earned approximately US$1,400 (almost double the salary male employees earn in the company's fabric production facility) plus productivity and quality incentives. This has empowered the nearly 350 women from poor families to become the prime income earners in the family (see case study in Section IV).

Many MIGA-supported projects also increased the employee families' quality of life by providing workers benefits such as housing, transportation, medical care, and schools for the workers' children.[15] Since these benefits are in the form of *direct* subsidies, higher disposable incomes also accrue to the workers. KAFCO and Crescent Greenwood, for example, have built a modern housing complex for their employees near their project sites, provide basic medical care for their employees and dependents, and offer free transportation to the project site, providing education to the employees' children as well. KAFCO's school is equipped with a science laboratory, a library, and is staffed with qualified teachers who provide education to 115 students. Crescent Greenwood has an outstanding school that is open to any child who wishes to enroll. To encourage the attendance of poor students, the company subsidizes their tuition fees (see case studies in Section IV).

Transfer of Knowledge

It is clear that lack of knowledge impedes the development process. By attracting foreign direct investment and participating in international trade, a host country can access and use new and existing techniques and skills that may not otherwise be locally available. For their part, foreign investors view the transfer of technology and managerial ability to their operations as essential to the proper implementation and the profitability of their investments. New knowledge and skills are initially transmitted by training a select group of workers and later disseminating it to the rest of the labor force. Transfer of knowledge also occurs through technology sales or licensing, or through labor mobility.[16] Fifteen out of the 25 projects monitored have facilitated transfer of knowledge.

> ### Example:
>
> **Motorola–Pakistan:** This cellular phone company introduced a more advanced digital technology in Pakistan that emits a clearer signal and is more compatible with computers and video transmissions than the analog cellular technology offered by other cellular phone companies in the country.

Knowledge and skills are also enhanced through adaptation, innovation, and dissemination of expertise. Innovation allows the project enterprise to develop a refined product or service that suits host country conditions. A company also becomes efficient by eliminating any distortions arising from the application of an "imported" technology.

---

[15] In some cases, these benefits help ease the burden on limited or severely constrained public services.

[16] Instances of knowledge transfer via labor mobility occur when employees of foreign subsidiaries join local firms or set up their own companies and take with them the technological, managerial, and marketing know-how that they have acquired.

> **Example:**
>
> **AFP Integra–Peru:** Building upon lessons learned from other private pension management companies operating in the region, AFP Integra manages a successful private pension fund in Peru. The company's experience in designing, marketing, and operating a private pension fund—initially in Lima—has enabled it to replicate, adapt, improve, and expand across the country. Subsequently, AFP Integra has provided financial advice and imparted expertise to other private pension fund management companies in Mexico, Colombia, and the Dominican Republic.

Financial sector projects that are expanding operations have relatively less value-added knowledge to transfer to their existing operation. ING Bank and Citibank N.A. in Argentina, Bank of America, and Crédit Agricole Indosuez, for example, have transferred the bulk of their know-how when they first initiated their operations and, thus, their ongoing contribution is not as great as inaugurating a new investment.

4. Diffused Effects

The Financial Sector and Capital Markets

Development of efficient financial and capital markets is crucial in mobilizing domestic savings, allocating capital efficiently for productive activities, and providing both savers and investors with a menu of alternatives affecting their financial decisions. Well-developed financial and capital markets enable financial intermediaries to allocate resources to economic activities that provide the highest marginal return on capital, a condition that is conducive to economic growth.

Foreign investment in the financial sector has both direct and indirect impacts on the host country. The host country directly benefits from foreign participation through the development of the local capital market. For example, a foreign investor can catalyze external funds, make more funds available to investors, lower the cost of capital to investors, promote competition, contribute to the resilience and stability of the local financial system, promote transparent policies, bring in new technology, and train local people in modern banking techniques. Indirect benefits include the creation of jobs, generation of export revenues, and institution building. As the host developing economy grows, and as incomes rise, the demand also rises for more complex financial services that sophisticated financial institutions can provide. The local economy also becomes more open and integrated with the rest of the world.

New Services and Financial Instruments

In Pakistan, MIGA provided guarantees to three banks. Their subsequent business expansion enabled them to offer new services and financial instruments. Société Générale's branch diversified its activities from interbank money market and foreign exchange transactions into corporate banking. Citibank N.A.'s branch was the first bank operating in the country to launch equity funds, private sector bonds denominated in local currency, Euro-convertible bonds, and floating-rate notes for the Pakistani government. Crédit Agricole Indosuez developed new financial instruments included in structured transactions.

In Argentina, Citibank N.A. extended existing banking activities to include advisory services, underwriting, and cash management. In Kazakhstan, ABN–AMRO Bank arranged and managed the country's launching of a US$200 million Eurobond and the creation of a financial consultancy unit that offers services to private and state-owned institutions. Recently, the government of Kazakhstan designated ABN–AMRO as one of the custodian banks for the newly privatized pension system. (At the same time, banks' geographical expansion will spread the availability of these services and financial instruments.)

Decreasing the Cost of Funds and Improving Credit Terms

MIGA also found that its support to financial projects helped lower the cost of funds, especially to small and medium-size enterprises. MIGA's support to Crédit Agricole Indosuez–Pakistan allowed the bank to offer one-year working capital loans during a period when most nonguaranteed funds were restricted to only three- to six-month terms. Similarly, Citibank N.A.–Pakistan was able to offer funding at rates below the ones prevailing in the local market. Banco de Boston's residential mortgage lending program in Argentina and BankBoston Leasing in Brazil are excellent examples of how loans were made available to middle-income families at lower interest rates and for a longer tenor.

Developing Local Capital Markets

The two aspects previously mentioned and the demonstration effect of some financial sector projects (e.g., ABN–AMRO Bank in Kazakhstan) indirectly contribute to the development of capital markets. However, there are some financial sector projects such as pension fund management that do so in a rather different way (see box below). The participation of pension fund managers in the stock market increases transaction and investment volumes and thus promotes the development of new and more sophisticated financial instruments.

> ## Box 4. Development of Local Capital Markets: AFP Integra, Peru
>
> In fiscal 1995, MIGA's extended a US$15 million guarantee contract to International Nederlanden Bank, N.V. (ING) to cover its 20-percent participation in AFP Integra, a Peruvian private pension fund manager. At the time the guarantee was issued, Peru was in the process of reforming its pension fund system.[17] MIGA's support to Integra AFP is a prime example of how foreign investment can help develop local capital markets.
>
> In 1993, Peru was the second Latin American country to privatize its pension system. The resulting increase in volume of "investable" funds spurred greater savings, injected new life to the Peruvian stock market, stimulated the demand for more new financial instruments, and increased the need for an efficient market to exchange these instruments. In turn, this dynamic evolutionary process stimulated a parallel modernization of the country's existing regulatory framework in order to effectively oversee market operations. The *Superintendencia de Administradoras Privadas de Fondos de Pensiones* was created by the government to regulate the activities of private pension fund managers.
>
> Between 1993 and 1997, the market capitalization of the Lima Stock Exchange increased from US$5 billion to about US$17 billion; primary securities offerings grew from about US$300 million to more than US$2.5 billion. In the pension fund's inaugural year, time deposits and government bonds were the only real instruments available. As of June 1998, the system's US$1.8 billion were invested in time deposits (25.2 percent); common shares (25.6 percent); and corporate bonds from nonfinancial institutions (19.5 percent). The remainder share included other financial instruments such as mortgage bills of exchange, labor shares, subordinated bonds, guaranteed promissory notes, leasing bonds, and commercial papers; less than 1 percent was invested in government bonds.
>
> AFP Integra is primarily owned by Aetna Pensiones Perú S.A. and Inversiones Wiese del Peru S.A, and other Peruvian investors. It has three agencies in Lima and 15 around the country. As of June 1998, AFP Integra had the second largest number of affiliates and had the largest share of the pension system's investment portfolio with 31.2 percent (US$530 million). Of these funds, about 44 percent were invested in instruments issued by the financial system (the portfolio includes 22 banks, six leasing companies, and two *fondos mutuos*); 55 percent was invested in private companies, and the remaining 1 percent in the government and the Central Bank.

Demonstration Effects

In some cases, a particular investment project may act as an example to both domestic and foreign investors, especially in countries experiencing recent political or economic crises. Some projects serve as models either because they were the first to venture into a risky or new market and/or because they do so with an innovative

---

[17] The IBRD extended a loan to the Peruvian government to reform the pension system; the IFC invested in one of the five *Administradoras Privadas de Fondos de Pensiones* (AFPs) in the system.

financial product or project structure. It is unquestionable that this demonstration effect has occurred in a number of MIGA-supported investments, and in some case it has been outstanding:

> ## Examples:
>
> **The Rain Forest Aerial Tram–Costa Rica:** The aerial tram is often cited as a model of how sensitive natural environments can be preserved and protected by nonintrusive usage. Several documentaries about the project have been filmed by European production companies and various foreign investors have tried to emulate the project's structure in similar endeavors in other Central American countries.
>
> **American Home Products–China:** The project, Suzhou Lederle Pharmaceutical Company, is considered a showcase operation by the Chinese government and is often used by officials for the purpose of site tours for other potential investors.
>
> **ABN–AMRO–Kazakhstan:** The bank's branch was the first modern financial institution to enter the Kazakh banking sector and opened the way for other institutions. In addition, it helped attract foreign investment in other sectors, since prospective foreign investors tend to consider, as part of their due diligence, the availability of reliable banking services.

Some projects are innovative and precedent-setting because they affect follow-up investments; contribute to decisions by the parent company to invest in other countries; and influence competitors' product development strategies. The results of this monitoring round identified several examples of this kind of positive demonstration effect (see case study: KAFCO Bangladesh in Section IV). Société Générale, a MIGA-supported branch bank project in Pakistan, for example, provided the know-how to open a new branch in Bangladesh. It is also important to obtain information about the use of a project enterprise's retained earnings, since they can be utilized to fund follow-up investments. If this is the case, the demonstration effect might include the opening of additional subsidiaries or affiliated companies in the host country.

Demonstration effects also often relate to changes in loan tenor and interest rates in the market attributable to the introduction of an innovative financial product. MIGA found conclusive evidence of such demonstration effects in financial projects which enhanced the competition, especially in consumer banking. This is the case for projects such as Banco de Boston's residential mortgage program in Argentina and BankBoston Leasing in Brazil. These projects set high standards that other institutions had to match to remain competitive. (The leasing market in Brazil currently exceeds US$12 billion compared to about US$6 billion in 1994. BankBoston Leasing has more than doubled its portfolio in the same time period. As a result, other institutions have become more aggressive.)

Table 5. Summary of Developmental Impacts of 25 MIGA-Assisted Projects

	Direct effects				Indirect effects			Diffused effects		
	Direct empl.	Human cap. invest.	Economic effects	Environ. effects	Downstream effects	Upstream effects	Transfer of knowledge	Soc./ Poverty alleviation	Demonst. effect	Fin./Cap markets
Manufacturing										
1. KAFCO, Bangladesh	+	+	+	+	✓✓	+	+	+	+	n.m.
2. American Home Products, China	✓✓	+	✓	✓✓	✓✓	✓✓	✓✓	✓✓	+	n.m.
3. Guardian Glass, Saudi Arabia	✓✓	✓✓	✓✓	✓✓	✓✓	✓✓	✓✓	✓	✓	n.m.
4. PCS Nitrogen-Arcadian, T&T	✓	+	+	✓✓	✓✓	+	+	✓✓	+	n.m.
5. Crescent Greenwood, Pakistan	+	+	✓✓	+	✓✓	+	+	+	+	n.m.
6. Komatsu Limited, Indonesia	✓✓	+	✓✓	✓✓	✓	✓	✓✓	✓✓	✓	n.m.
7. Volvo Perú S.A., Peru	✓✓	✓✓	✓	✓	+	✓✓	✓✓	✓✓	✓	n.m.
Financial Services										
1. Société Générale, Pakistan	+	+	✓	n.m.	✓✓	✓✓	+	n.m.	✓✓	✓✓
2. ING Bank, Brazil	u.t.	✓✓	✓	n.m.	✓✓	u.t.	✓	n.m.	✓	✓
3. Citibank N.A., Argentina	u.t.	✓✓	✓✓	n.m.	✓✓	u.t.	✓	n.m.	✓	✓✓
4. Crédit Agricole Indosuez, Pakistan	u.t.	✓✓	✓	n.m.	u.t.	u.t.	✓	n.m.	✓	✓
5. Citibank N.A., Pakistan	u.t.	✓✓	✓	n.m.	u.t.	u.t.	✓	n.m.	✓✓	✓✓
6. Bank of America, Pakistan	✓✓	✓✓	✓	n.m.	u.t.	u.t.	✓	n.m.	✓	✓
7. ING Bank, Argentina	u.t.	✓✓	✓	n.m.	u.t.	u.t.	✓	n.m.	✓	✓
8. BankBoston Leasing, Brazil	✓	✓✓	✓	n.m.	+	u.t.	✓✓	n.m.	✓✓	✓✓
9. BankBoston NA, Brazil	u.t.	✓✓	✓	n.m.	u.t.	u.t.	✓	n.m.	✓	✓
10. Banco de Boston, Argentina	+	+	✓✓	n.m.	+	✓✓	+	n.m.	+	+
11. ABN AMRO Bank, Kazakhstan	+	+	✓✓	n.m.	✓✓	✓✓	+	n.m.	+	+
12. Citibank N.A., Turkey	✓✓	✓✓	✓	n.m.	✓✓	u.t.	✓	n.m.	✓	✓
13. ING Bank/AFP Integra, Peru	✓✓	+	✓✓	n.m.	✓✓	u.t.	✓✓	n.m.	✓✓	+
14. Citibank N.A./AFP Profuturo, Peru	✓✓	+	✓✓	n.m.	✓✓	u.t.	✓✓	n.m.	✓✓	+
Others										
1. Rain Forest Aerial Tram, Costa Rica	✓✓	✓✓	✓✓	+	✓✓	✓✓	✓✓	✓	+	n.m.
2. MultiServ International, RSA	✓✓	✓✓	✓	✓	✓	✓	✓✓	✓	✓	n.m.
3. SAS Partners/Gate Gourmet, Turkey	✓	+	✓✓	✓✓	✓✓	✓✓	+	n.m.	✓✓	n.m.
4. Motorola, Pakistan	✓✓	✓✓	✓	n.m.	✓✓	✓	+	✓	✓	n.m.

+ = effect is outstanding ; ✓✓ = effect is beneficial; ✓ = effect is minimal; u.t. = effect is not traced; n.m. = effect is not measured.

Explanatory Notes to Table 5

A. ***Direct effects:*** Clear and direct causal connection between the MIGA-guaranteed investment and the following:

- **Direct employment** = Defined as the number of employees the enterprise hires specifically because of the investment (for a greenfield operation) or, number of new jobs created as a result of the MIGA-guaranteed investment (for expansion or privatization).

- **Human capital investment** = Measured by the access to training of both existing and new employees or in certain cases, nonemployees, the range of training courses offered, the average number of man-hours devoted to training, and any evidence of increase in productivity as a result of training. This category also considered presence of Technical Agreements or TQM programs as evidence of "human capital investment."

- **Economic effects** = Refer to balance of payment effects (i.e., export revenues generation, import substitution effects) tax revenue generation, support of macro or sectoral economic program/policies, and the leverage effect of MIGA's investment. For financial projects, the category also considers its effect on generation of domestic savings in the economy.

- **Environmental effects** = Refer to project enterprise's adherence to environmentally sound and sustainable practices. Attention is particularly paid to the enterprise's compliance with World Bank Environmental Guidelines plus any ISO certification.

B. ***Indirect effects:*** By-products of the project's business activities; the causal connection to the investment is more difficult to measure, such as:

- **Downstream effects** = Refer to the benefit to other businesses or economic agents that utilize the project's output as an input in their production process.

- **Upstream effects** = Refer to the benefits to suppliers of goods and services (e.g., subcontractors) used in the project's production process.

- **Transfer of knowledge** = Knowledge is defined in terms of technical knowledge (i.e., knowledge of technologies and its potentials) and socioeconomic knowledge. The following elements are considered: creation and acquisition, adaptation and diffusion, and use of knowledge.

- **Social development/Poverty alleviation** = Includes the following elements:
  - ➢ higher wages than country and industry average, as a measure of increases in employees' and their families' net worth;

> generous worker benefits, as a form of direct subsidy and, in case of IDA countries, provision of social goods and services that the government could not otherwise provide. It specifically measures increase in workers' welfare;

> greater number of women hired; and

> provision of social infrastructure directly for the project's employees and to the surrounding community.

C. *Diffused effects:* Impacts that influence many socioeconomic entities before its effects are felt in the host country's overall economy.

- **Demonstration effects** = Refer to the project enterprise serving as an example or model to both domestic and foreign investors. For example, the project was the first to venture into a risky or new market, or, the project introduced an innovative product or service that contributed to the decision by the parent company and/or its competitors to invest in other projects.

- **Financial sector/Capital markets** = Refer primarily to the effect of the financial sector projects in terms of developing new services and financial instruments, decreasing the cost of funds and improving credit terms, and spurring the development of the local capital market (i.e., establishing the stock market, increasing the volume of investable funds and creating demand for more new financial instruments).

IV. Case Studies

In the course of the evaluation process, an unanticipated trove of information on one project, KAFCO in Bangladesh, encouraged MIGA staff to conduct a more in-depth analysis of the developmental impact of this project than was originally envisaged. (This depth of analysis was not planned to be undertaken until a later phase of the MIGA evaluation program.) The report on KAFCO proved to be a useful means to explore the types of impacts that a private investment has in a developing country. Later, two more projects in other sectors were selected to broaden the conceptual framework developed for the KAFCO projects. The availability of data for such studies was an important consideration as well as the cooperation from the investors in providing additional information. The case studies, however, are not designed to be definitive assessments of the projects' impacts on the economic development of their respective host countries; but they are comprehensive treatments of their most important developmental effects.

These three case studies were undertaken during fiscal years 1997–98 (the specific date is noted for each of them). Therefore, it should be remembered that the analyses and conclusions in those studies correspond to the information available at that time. The benefit of retaining the integrity of these papers, and not updating them, resides in exposing the original information found as a result of the evaluation process.

Thus, this section presents three case studies about the developmental impacts of the following MIGA-assisted projects: (1) KAFCO, the construction and operation of a major ammonia and granular urea processing plant in Bangladesh, (2) Banco de Boston, a residential mortgage program in Argentina, and (3) Crescent Greenwood, Ltd., the construction and operation of a fully integrated garment production facility in Pakistan.

A. Karnaphuli Fertilizer Company, Ltd. (KAFCO), Bangladesh[18]

Introduction

The purpose of this report is to describe the developmental impacts of the Karnaphuli Fertilizer Company, Ltd. (KAFCO), project in Bangladesh. The effects of the KAFCO project in Bangladesh have been significant by nearly every measure. After the project is introduced, KAFCO's developmental impacts are examined. After a brief discussion of the general impact of the project, its impact on employees' family income, specifically concerning job creation and contribution to social infrastructure, is ad-

---

[18] This case-study is an abridged version of a report prepared by Ms. Ethel I. Tarazona in December 1996 under the general supervision of Mr. Gerald T. West.

– 37 –

dressed. KAFCO's introduction of new technology is discussed together with training provided to its employees. Spillover effects are evaluated, including both upstream and downstream effects. Following a discussion of KAFCO's market impact, its economic impacts are evaluated at the aggregate level. KAFCO's demonstration effects are identified in the context of its modern technology and innovative financial structure. A final section is devoted to the project's environmental impact.

Project Background

In fiscal 1991, MIGA issued two contracts of guarantee totaling US$19.8 million covering the Marubeni and Chiyoda Corporations' loan guaranties issued in favor of commercial banks lending to KAFCO. Subsequently, in fiscal 1993, MIGA issued two additional contracts of guarantee totaling US$32.19 million covering Marubeni's and Chiyoda's shareholder loans to KAFCO. MIGA insured the guarantee holders against the risks of Transfer Restriction, Expropriation, and War and Civil Disturbance.

The project involves the construction and operation of a major ammonia and granular urea processing plant at the mouth of the Karnaphuli River near Chittagong City (approximately 200 kilometers southeast of Dhaka). KAFCO utilizes local natural gas to produce international quality urea and ammonia for export. This enterprise—with a cost of approximately US$516 million—represents the largest joint venture foreign investment in Bangladesh to date. The plant utilizes world-class fertilizer technology, and it was designed to have an ammonia production capacity of 495,000 tons p.a., and a urea production capacity of 569,000 tons p.a. About 330,000 tons of the ammonia was intended to be used as an input for urea production, with the balance being exported along with all the urea output.

Box 5. Development Highlights: KAFCO, Bangladesh

- Strong investment in human capital with an aggressive training program for more than 1,000 participants in one year;
- Strong backward linkages with an annual expenditure of US$32 million in local inputs;
- Strong forward linkages with the creation and/or expansion of many businesses;
- A positive technical impact in introducing new fertilizer technology;
- Market impact in introducing Bangladeshi ammonia as an export product and improving urea for export;
- Paying US$3.56 million in annual duties and taxes, increasing the tax base, employing about 2,000 workers for the construction phase, and creating more than 600 permanent jobs;
- Extensive provision of a complete social infrastructure for its employees, including housing, school, transportation, medical services and recreation facilities; and
- Careful management of environmental impacts.

– 38 –

Initial Estimates of Developmental Impacts

At the time MIGA issued its guarantees, the project was considered to be consistent with the government of Bangladesh's objective of developing natural resource-based and export-oriented industries. The project was deemed to be very attractive to Bangladesh because it would (a) involve large-scale, foreign private investors, which Bangladesh had trouble attracting, (b) create a major industrial exporter and foreign exchange earner, and (c) provide means of converting the country's ample reserves of low-cost natural gas into an export commodity.

It was further anticipated that the project would enhance the image of Bangladesh's investment environment and thus encourage more foreign investment in the country. During its first 15 years of operations, it was anticipated that the project would contribute about US$1 billion in foreign exchange to Bangladesh's economy, after foreign dividend remittances and debt service. The project's operations would allow Bangladesh to diversify its export income and move away from traditional exports of commodities such as tea and jute. In addition, the government would receive dividend and tax income of some US$370 million over the project's life. The local gas company also would benefit from significantly increased sales.

It was estimated that the project would employ some 2,000 people during the construction phase and create 835 new permanent jobs. Stamicarbon (a Dutch investor) would conduct training for engineers and technical staff at its existing training centers in Bangladesh, and Chiyoda would provide training for KAFCO's personnel both locally and outside of Bangladesh.

Ex-Post Evaluation of Economic and Developmental Impacts

In September 1996, a MIGA Guarantee Officer visited the project site and met with KAFCO managers and staff to gather information that would provide a basis to assess the impact of the project. He was equipped with a detailed Project Monitoring Questionnaire and had been briefed on the type of information that was needed for this analysis.

The KAFCO staff were very cooperative with MIGA's efforts to evaluate the project's developmental impact. Managers at the corporate office in Dhaka and staff at the project site were extremely helpful in providing information on their respective areas of operation, and the MIGA representative was provided with unlimited access to the project site. As a result of his visit, KAFCO completed the detailed project monitoring questionnaire, and provided MIGA with additional information on the financial, technical, environmental, and staff development aspects of the project. This Monitoring Report is based primarily on this information. (World Bank Country Officers and the Resident Mission were also consulted.)

KAFCO had commenced production of ammonia on December 15, 1994, and urea on December 28, 1994, after a delay of 13 months from the planned start date. KAFCO attributed this delay mainly to the government's tardiness in issuing guarantees for KAFCO's export credit; funds were not disbursed by the lenders, and payments to the contractors could not be made. As a result, the contractors suspended their construction work for one year. The delay also caused an increase in construction costs.

From December 15, 1994, to August 31, 1996, the plant produced 608,615 MT of ammonia, 595,953 MT of urea, and 263,058 MT of excess ammonia for urea production. The first shipment of liquid ammonia was in January 1995, of bulk urea in April, 1995, and of bagged urea in June 1996. The first shipment (12,000 MT) of refrigerated ammonia was sent from the KAFCO docks to California in January 1995.

At the time the first MIGA contracts were issued, the World Bank (IDA) was planning to finance a gas pipeline project in 1991/93 with the objective of increasing the availability of gas to KAFCO and other industrial users. The pipeline, which was completed and inaugurated in early May 1997, will assure the plant of the necessary gas supply (the plant requires approximately 58 million cubic feet of gas per day).

Economic Effects

KAFCO was the first company in Bangladesh to develop ammonia as an export product, and improved the quality of urea for export. In this way, it contributed to Bangladesh's declared objective of creating major industrial (resource-based) export products. The project was one of seven urea plants in Bangladesh and represented an estimated 20 percent of the nation's total urea production capacity. Also the urea industry in Bangladesh benefited from KAFCO's entry, as it has introduced productivity enhancements and better product quality and, thus, introduced a "right incentive"[19] for improvements in other products in the market. Both products, ammonia and urea, helped to move Bangladesh's exports away from dependency on basic commodities.

Though the project intended to export 100 percent of its output, there was a possibility that KAFCO may sell part of its urea output in the domestic market. Because of a serious supply-demand gap, the government asked KAFCO to help bridge the urea production shortfall. Even though KAFCO agreed to do so on international terms, this was an unanticipated positive effect on the country, since it would be contributing to breaking supply bottlenecks in the Bangladeshi urea market.

KAFCO had several significant impacts on the economy of Bangladesh. Two of the direct macroeconomic effects are its contributions to the country's export earnings and to the government's tax revenues. KAFCO provided a useful mechanism to convert gas into export earnings; the project generated US$90.84 million in export revenues in 1995, or the equivalent of 3 percent of the total merchandise exports of the country. In 1995, this amount was comparable to the total export earnings from the two traditional export commodities, raw jute and tea, in that year (US$99.6 million).[20]

---

[19] A World Bank Country Study addresses the problems associated with quality deterioration in the Bangladeshi industry. It describes a set of market disincentives to improve quality of products, including "competition" among producers to lower costs by reducing quality ("Bangladesh: From Stabilization to Growth," The World Bank, 1995).

[20] As estimated by World Bank Staff, Country Operations Division, Country Department I, South Asia Region, CAS, September 1995.

– 40 –

The government of Bangladesh benefited from KAFCO's contribution to revenues. The company enjoyed concessions on custom duties and taxes on imports during the construction phase, and a tax holiday of 9 years agreed to by the government is currently being reconsidered by the relevant tax authority. Nonetheless, in 1995 it paid to the government approximately US$3.56 million in other taxes and duties. The government also will be receiving dividends when the debt-to-equity ratio is one to one; KAFCO estimates this target will be reached by the year 2002.

One of the more important macroeconomic effects of this project was the expansion of Bangladesh's tax base. Because of the creation and/or expansion of companies that supply KAFCO with production inputs and the companies that indirectly serve KAFCO's needs, the corporate tax base increased. Likewise, all new employees of those companies are subject to income tax, thus increasing the personal income tax base. In addition, sales of new products and services contribute to new tax revenues.

Investment in Human Capital

When the plant was designed, there was some skepticism about the availability of highly skilled workers who would be able to manage the plant's modern technology. The results of this monitoring trip are positive in this regard. KAFCO recruited high-potential workers and trained them by investing time and resources in an elaborate training program. The accomplishments for a single 12-month period (August 1995 to July 1996) are impressive (see Figure 9). There were 1,024 participants in those training courses (an average of 1.7 courses per worker in one year). Clearly, the company invested heavily in human capital, especially in the early stages of the project. In addition, there was an ongoing training program equivalent to 122 employee months.

Figure 9. KAFCO's Training Program
(August 1995–July 1996)

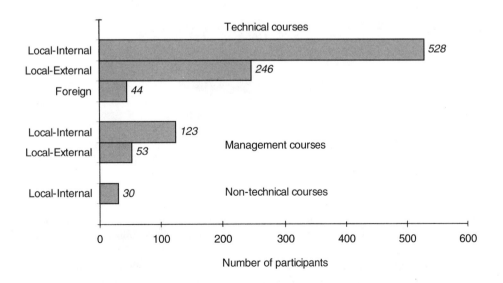

KAFCO's training programs exist both locally and abroad, encompassing technical, management, and support staff. At the time the evaluation took place, KAFCO had already sent overseas 44 participants (mostly managers) to be trained in Denmark, Holland, Indonesia, Japan, Pakistan, and Singapore.

The range of in-house training subjects was equally impressive.[21] Outside courses offered by the company included: basic training for trainees (a customized training program); automatic logic operation and sequential process control; mechanical maintenance; industrial accident and safety management; personnel management; management of human resources and organizational development; public relations; chlorine cylinder handling and transportation; total quality management; computer courses (C++ and Excel); office management; engineering management; executive development; maintenance of rotating machines; spectrometric methods of analysis; supervisory welding training; diagnosis of machine problems; induction motor; and operation and maintenance of microcomputers.

Direct Employment Effects

As anticipated, KAFCO employed about 2,000 workers during the four-year construction phase. In 1996, the company employed 602 workers on a permanent basis (including managerial, professional and labor) (see Figure 10). Out of the 602 employees, there were only five expatriates. More than 95 percent of the management positions were held by nationals. In addition to the permanent positions, KAFCO employed another 320 workers through contractors. In aggregate, there are more than 900 families that directly benefited from KAFCO's operations in Bangladesh.

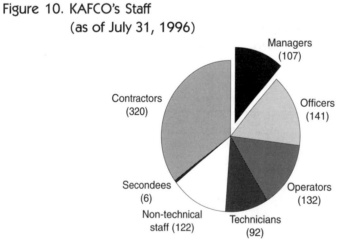

Figure 10. KAFCO's Staff (as of July 31, 1996)

---

[21] The courses offered in-house include leakage in the plant and preventive actions; safety equipment; first aid; introduction to plant operations; fire alarm; siren test and mock drill; usage and care of canteen equipment; breathing protection system; safety awareness and personnel protective equipment; breathing apparatus; urea plant; providing a quality service; occupational hazards and prevention; basic fire fighting; urea plant refresher course; practical training on OHS, orientation

Environmental Effect

Before the first contracts of guarantee were issued in 1990, an Environmental Review was undertaken. The IFC, MIGA's Environmental Advisor, reviewed the documentation and found the project to be in consonance with World Bank Guidelines. However, at that time, KAFCO was also required to conduct a Hazard Study and submit it to MIGA.

KAFCO supplied MIGA with a Hazard Analysis, undertaken in December 1994, and a Study Supplement of March 1995. The IFC reviewed these analyses for consonance with World Bank Guidelines at the time the contracts were issued as well as with current guidelines. The IFC reported that the Hazard Analysis was, in general terms, "following acceptable principles for preparation of a hazard assessment," but at the same time, it raised some questions on the assumptions used as a basis for the study and suggested that a new Hazard Analysis be undertaken.

In response to MIGA's suggestion, KAFCO voluntarily prepared a new Hazard Analysis, submitted to MIGA in April 1997, which takes into consideration the suggestions made by the IFC for new modeling (and a set of consequence calculations) for an accidental ammonia leakage from the plant. The new study was reviewed by the IFC Environmental Division and found to be of high quality and demonstrated "good professionalism." The IFC concurred with the emergency response system recommendations made in the study and supported their implementation. KAFCO found the results to be very useful and made several changes in its emergency response system.

As stated when the contracts of guarantees were signed, KAFCO has built-in facilities for treatment of effluents. The company undertook an aggressive plan of environmental management and workers' safety. Staff are routinely trained in industrial accident and safety management, safety equipment, and occupational hazards and prevention. Danish experts were recruited to conduct the seminars on occupational health and safety.

Social Development

KAFCO has built a very comprehensive social infrastructure for its local staff. The housing complex, valued at US$8 million, is located two kilometers from the project site. KAFCO turned a sparsely populated area into a modern satellite community to accommodate most of its employees and their families. The housing complex was designed and built by local architects and contractors in a record time of one year. The company undertook an expansion to the housing complex, consisting of four buildings and a mosque. The expansion was valued at US$1.2 million.

---

and maintenance of TADANO cranes; CO_2 fire suppression system; use and calibration of sound level meters; orientation training for process officers; urea plant training programs for process officers; power generation; urea synthesis and granulation unit; introductory training for KAFCO security inspectors; and distributed control systems. KAFCO also offers on-the-job training courses such as training on standard operating procedure (SOP) for the ammonia and urea plants.

- *Housing:* Employees and their families lived in an impressive residential complex of 233 modern family apartments equipped with furniture and appliances. These apartments are located in modern five-story buildings with all services. The expansion accommodates 40 more families of employees. There is also a bachelor hostel accommodation for 80 persons, and a guest house.

- *Transportation:* Staff are transported to the project site by KAFCO buses, while managers are provided cars. Transportation is also provided to and from the city of Chittagong.

- *Medical:* Basic medical care is provided to employees and their families. The five-bed health clinic in the colony has a full-time doctor, several nurses, and fairly advanced medical equipment, including an x-ray machine. Employees and their dependents are also provided with preventive and prenatal care.

- *Education:* Education up to the 10th grade is provided to employees' children. The school facility has 15 teachers providing education to 115 students. The school is equipped with a science laboratory, a library and sports facilities. Students are granted uniforms, books and other supplies. KAFCO has plans to train teachers to enable the expansion of the school up to grade 12 and to offer education to 600 students in the future.

- *Religious Center:* With the expansion of the housing colony, the company has added a mosque for the use of its employees.

- *Recreation:* The company has built sports facilities (e.g., tennis courts) for its employees, a staff club, and a corporate club with full services.

Poverty Alleviation

In addition to creating jobs, KAFCO increased families' net worth. It was reported that KAFCO paid its employees two to four times more than comparable wages and salaries in Bangladesh. The payment of higher wages and salaries was a crucial factor in attracting high-quality, mostly younger, staff. This staff also benefited from having a career path with potential for future growth, advancement, and higher income.

KAFCO's impact on its workers' income extends beyond their salaries. The company provides its employees with basic services such as housing, transportation, medical care, and schooling. As a result of these direct subsidies, an unusually high percentage of family income is disposable.

Transfer of Knowledge

The plant was built with state-of-the-art technology; KAFCO adopted the Haldor Topsoe ammonia process, Stamicarbon urea process, Hydro-Agri urea granulation process, and UOP CO_2 removal process. Both Haldor Topsoe and Stamicarbon are regarded as premier companies in fertilizer production technology. The Haldor Topsoe-designed ammonia unit employs the most modern energy-saving features. The introduction of this technology represented a milestone for Bangladesh. In the short-term, it had important effects in producing urea and ammonia more efficiently (including resource flows and resource productivity), and in increasing the level of technological skills of its workers. The introduction of this technology created economies of scale, decreasing average costs and thus making the plant more efficient to operate. In the longer term, this new technology may be adopted by the industry in Bangladesh. Other fertilizer firms also benefited by KAFCO's voluntary sharing of technology through workshops and training to workers.

Upstream and Downstream Effects

KAFCO estimated that 77 percent of production inputs (goods and services) are purchased locally. Local procurement of goods and services, including natural gas and process chemicals, during 1995–96 was US$32 million, of which the state-owned gas company received US$28 million.

Other local companies benefited from KAFCO by supplying chemicals, lubricants, greases, and packing materials; they have received an estimated US$653,000 in 1995–96. In addition, the company estimated that it had spent US$1.3 million on purchases related to administrative expenses. In 1996, KAFCO employed (through contractors) 80 temporary workers to bag urea, 200 security agents, and 40 cleaning workers. KAFCO estimated that in 1995–96 it has spent US$1.98 million on contract services. This expenditure on local inputs (goods and services), in turn, had a multiplier effect in terms of generation of jobs, raising incomes, increasing spending, and contribution to tax revenues.

Downstream effects are also important and, in some cases, the effects of foreign investment on companies not directly related to the project (or to the production) are particularly beneficial to the country. In the case of KAFCO, many businesses benefited from the project; they include a bank, insurance companies, and a job placement agency. It is notable that many small businesses emerged outside the project site to service the needs of the employees and their families (e.g., barbers, cleaners, small retail shops, etc.) The multiplier effects of these businesses are numerous, including the generation of jobs and contribution to tax revenues.

Demonstration Effect

Although the fertilizer industry is not new to Bangladesh, KAFCO served as a model for other investors. It was the first privately owned fertilizer company in the country and was a model to other companies for its advanced technology, product quality, human resources management, and investment in social infrastructure. The KAFCO project has, from MIGA's perspective, clearly enhanced Bangladesh's foreign investment image; the atmosphere for private investment improved over the years following the investment. The project was cited in a World Bank Country Study[22] as one of two most important developments in attracting foreign capital that has occurred in Bangladesh (the other development being the Dhaka Export Processing Zones). The project is viewed by World Bank officials working with Bangladesh as a showcase for foreign investment in the country that sends an important, positive signal to foreign investors.

As the largest joint venture in the country at the time, the project demonstrated that Bangladesh could provide a positive environment for foreign investment. Other firms with plans to invest in the country were reassured by KAFCO's example. Indeed, an advertisement by The Bangladeshi Board of Investment publicized the success of foreign companies like Chiyoda and Marubeni (KAFCO investors) in Bangladesh for the purpose of attracting other companies. (Bangladesh's MIGA membership was also cited in the advertisement as one additional attraction for foreign investment.)

The project also provided an example of project structuring. The financing of the KAFCO project was a complex international operation in the capital markets, and the first of its kind for Bangladesh. KAFCO's financing earned the "Deal of 1990" award from *Trade Finance* magazine.[23] Until the deal was completed, there had been no availability in the capital markets for Bangladeshi risk. Since no single source of finance was adequate to cover KAFCO's funding requirements, the package introduced limited-recourse commercial project financing in parallel with export credit financing and insurance.

The project was a joint collaboration between four semigovernmental agencies and four private companies. Investors included the Bangladesh Chemical Industrial Corporation (BCIC), owned by the government of Bangladesh; KAFCO Japan, a special purpose company owned by Japan's Overseas Economic Cooperation Fund; Chiyoda and Marubeni Corporations; Denmark's Haldor Topsoe; the United Kingdom's Commonwealth Development Corporation; Denmark's International Fund for Developing Countries; and Holland's Stamicarbon b.v. Financing for the project included loans from the Japanese Export Import Bank (JEXIM); the Italian Export Credit Agency (SACE); the Commonwealth Development Corporation (CDC); the Romanian Export Credit Agency; commercial banks; and shareholders. The project also made ground-breaking use of investment insurance provided by five organizations: ECGD of the United Kingdom, MITI of Japan, OPIC of the United States, SACE of Italy, and MIGA.

Thus, the financing package was not only original and complex, but it was also successful in its catalytic efforts to involve foreign companies, development agencies, institutional investors, export credit agencies, and investment insurers in a large-scale project in Bangladesh. For many, it was the first time they had seriously considered a project in Bangladesh.

---

[22] "Bangladesh: From Stabilization to Growth," A World Bank Country Study, The World Bank, Washington DC, 1995, p. 74.

[23] Trade Finance, December 1990, pp. 36–41.

B. Banco de Boston, Argentina[24]

Introduction

The developmental impacts of the fiscal 1993 MIGA-supported residential mortgage program of Banco de Boston in Argentina have been notable with considerable multiplier effects in the Argentine economy. The results of the evaluation exercise confirmed that the expected developmental impacts of the program have been realized, and have generally exceeded MIGA's expectations when it issued the guarantee. It was also confirmed that this investment will continue to have much more impact in the future.

This project evaluation will begin by introducing the project; subsequently, Argentina's economic condition is discussed together with a brief analysis of the country's housing sector. The IBRD's role in supporting Argentina's economic reforms is noted with emphasis on its involvement in the financial and housing sectors. MIGA's basis for extending its guarantee is analyzed within this context. After a review of the initial estimations of the developmental effects of the investment, the current project status is discussed and an analysis is presented of the ex-post economic and developmental impacts.

Project Background

In fiscal 1993, MIGA extended a US$50 million guarantee to the First National Bank of Boston (now BankBoston) of the United States for an investment in its branch in Buenos Aires, Argentina, to create a long-term investment mortgage program. MIGA provided coverage to the investor against Transfer Restriction and Expropriation of Funds.

Banco de Boston, the project enterprise, was established in Argentina in 1917 and is one of the oldest foreign banks operating in the country, as well as the country's fourth largest bank overall in terms of assets. It provides a full range of banking services through its 43 offices around the country (at the time the guarantee was issued there were 34). In 1996, the last year for which figures are available, Banco de Boston reported net earnings of US$33.5 million, and had assets totaling approximately US$4 billion (compared with US$31.6 million and $682.7 million reported respectively in 1993).

Rationale for the MIGA Loan Guarantee

Banco de Boston had experimented with mortgage financing prior to receiving the MIGA-insured funds but had been obliged, because of a lack of longer term funds in Argentina, to borrow domestically on a short-term basis and to lend on

---

[24] This case-study is an abridged version of a report prepared by Ms. Ethel I. Tarazona in December 1997 under the general supervision of Mr. Gerald T. West.

a longer term basis. The result was a mismatch of maturities and interest rates of mortgages and deposits, which created a substantial interest rate risk for financial institutions. It was foreseen that the only feasible way Banco de Boston could get long-term fixed-rate funds was from its parent company in the United States.

The MIGA loan guarantee was viewed as particularly important to the consummation of this investment. Officials from BankBoston, the parent company, reported to MIGA that headquarters was unwilling to risk more exposure in Argentina without political risk insurance (the Overseas Private Investment Corporation of the U.S. declined to participate in the project due to capacity constraints). BankBoston's main concern was the then-unsettled state of the Argentine economy. As discussed in the preceding section, until 1990, there was declining confidence in the domestic currency and other financial assets. Successive episodes of hyperinflation and outright asset confiscation in the early 1980s and later in 1990 discouraged investors and depositors from holding domestic financial assets. At the time when the guarantee was issued, Argentina had emerged from the severe economic crisis of 1989–90 and adopted the Convertibility Plan in 1991. However, the effects of this plan were still uncertain and investors felt insecure about the government's continuing adherence to it.

Macroeconomic Background

In order to assess the impact of Banco de Boston's mortgage program, it is important to note the changes in the economic and political setting in Argentina during the 1990–97 period. Since the condition of the Argentine housing sector at the time the guarantee was issued is relevant to this analysis, those conditions are also discussed. Another important element in this context was the IBRD's role in supporting the economic reforms in Argentina. Special attention is given to the IBRD activities in the banking and housing sectors during this period as they pertain to this MIGA-assisted mortgage program.

As a result of decades of mismanagement and misguided economic policies, the Argentine economy in the late 1980s was overburdened by its external debt and recurring bouts of hyperinflation. President Menem, elected in 1989, carried out a comprehensive economic restructuring program that began putting the nation on a path of stable, sustainable growth. As its centerpiece, the Convertibility Plan was implemented in April of 1991, an innovative plan which restructured Argentina's economic landscape. Since then, the Argentine peso has been traded at par with the U.S. dollar. As a result, inflation dropped to its lowest level in 20 years; from extreme hyperinflation in the previous years, it moved relatively quickly to an annual inflation of less than four percent by 1994.

Argentineans responded to price stability by repatriating flight capital and investing in domestic industry. As a result of increasing inflows of foreign capital and strong domestic consumption, output and productivity increases were remarkable during the 1991–94 period, with an annual real GDP growth rate of 8.9 percent.

However, in the following year, the Mexican peso crisis erupted, undermining investor confidence and triggering capital outflows, resulting in a substantial recession. Soon after, higher commodity prices, a commendable adherence to the Convertibility Plan, and a strong demand for the country's exports resulted in the beginnings of a substantial recovery. Although unemployment remained high at about 16 percent, it was declining from a peak of 18 percent reached during the crisis.

The Housing Sector

The Argentine housing sector had been facing many problems for decades. With Argentina's population of 33 million, the housing deficit was estimated to be 2.5 million units with capital requirements of US$12 to US$15 billion. A 1988 World Bank housing study reported that during the last 15 years, the availability of private resources in this sector had decreased gradually from 75 percent in 1975 to less than 50 percent of the total investment in 1987. House construction decreased from 150,000 units in 1975 to a little over 80,000 units in past years, which was not sufficient to keep abreast of new household formation, estimated at 130,000. An UNDP study of 1987 demonstrated that the gap between demand and supply for affordable low-income housing had been widening for a number of years as a result of the disappearance of a long-term capital market for housing funds and the insufficient supply of government-supported housing.

A World Bank report noted that by 1991 the housing conditions had not improved. According to the 1991 census, 32.6 percent of all Argentineans still lived in overcrowded or physically inadequate housing. Housing specialists within the bank argued that housing conditions in Argentina were getting worse with the housing deficit growing by 115,000 units per annum. This was due to the fact that only 100,000 new houses were built each year, while 90,000 units of the existing stock become "unlivable" and 125,000 additional units were needed to meet the growing demand of newly formed households.[25]

Home mortgages were not new to Argentina. Banco Hipotecario Nacional (BHN or National Housing Bank), had served as an important pillar of the government's housing programs since the 1940s. BHN generally provided housing and construction credit to middle-income households. Extremely high inflation and low deposit mobilization caused the Central Bank to become BHN's sole financier by the late 1980s. The increasing emphasis on social concerns provoked a weakening of BHN's financial status; inflation indexation of the mortgage loan portfolio drove payments to unaffordable levels. Several concessionary adjustments negotiated with the borrowers, including interest rate reductions and maturity extensions, led to portfolio yields below funding costs. Despite these concessions, collections performance did not improve and lingered around 75 percent of amounts falling due.

---

[25] World Bank, "Argentina: From Insolvency to Growth," A World Bank Country Study, Washington DC, 1993.

Complementarity with the World Bank Group

The IBRD has been a strong supporter of the ambitious Argentine reform program launched by the Menem administration.[26] Through a series of sector loans, an intensive program of economic and sector work, and adjustment lending, the bank aimed to give the proper support to consolidate the macroeconomic reforms and deepen their impact. It also aimed to make the reforms more permanent by strengthening Argentina's weakened financial institutions and by fostering the developing of the private sector with particular attention to its resource mobilization and intermediation roles.

The Argentine financial sector received significant attention from the World Bank. In 1993, a financial sector adjustment loan of US$400 million was extended to reduce the role of the state in the financial sector, strengthen the banking sector and its supervisory framework, and provide resources for Argentina's debt and debt service reduction arrangement. It also helped identify the problems and constraints hindering financial development. At the time of the loan, Argentina's financial sector was marked by steady decline in its resource mobilization capabilities. Public sector financial institutions had grown to dominate the financial landscape. For decades, the Central Bank had been the ultimate source of funds for the public sector and subsidies for the private sector. Moreover, private financial institutions were undermined by the poor macroeconomic and financial policies pursued by the successive governments. In 1995, the IBRD extended a Bank Reform Loan with the objective of supporting the government's bank reform program. The program intended to help consolidate the fragmented private banking sector, improve the financial structure of the distressed banking sector, and restore confidence in the banking system, which was badly battered by the events following the Mexican financial crisis. The results of these IBRD efforts were positive. With the bank's support, the government of Argentina succeeded in stabilizing the financial sector, privatizing more than a dozen public banks, restoring confidence in the financial sector, and restraining the outflow of capital.

The IBRD's First Housing Sector Project in Argentina, which preceded the Convertibility Plan, did not succeed as planned. The project failed to achieve its objectives because of inadequate design, and Argentina's volatile political and economic situation through 1991 contributed to its failure. Its failure was an indication of the multitude of problems that an ambitious public sector project could have. It also served to illustrate that, when juxtaposed to the Banco de Boston Mortgage Program, the private sector, backed by MIGA, could help to relieve an acute problem at far lesser cost to both the Bank Group and Argentina. Needless to say, this program was feasible once the overall economic situation was stabilized with extensive IBRD support for privatization and other key structural reforms. As noted above, this stability was a precondition for the success of the MIGA-assisted Banco de Boston investment.

---

[26] The IBRD is currently emphasizing supporting ongoing government efforts to consolidate structural reforms, to strengthen the social safety net underpinning the Convertibility Plan, and to begin tackling second generation issues, such as access to international private capital markets.

Case Studies

Box 6. Development Highlights: Banco de Boston, Argentina

- Increased ability of Argentine citizens to own their own homes;
- Stimulation of competition in the mortgage market with important benefits to the consumers (including longer loan terms and lower interest rates);
- Increased employment: 200 new employees now work directly with the mortgage program and many more employees work in other supporting activities;
- Substantial investment in human capital by training staff on the latest credit techniques;
- Boost of the construction industry—one of Argentina's fastest growing sectors and an important generator of employment;
- The demonstration effect of this precedent-setting initiative has been significant throughout the country's entire banking sector; other banks have followed its lead and introduced new mortgage products in the market;
- Contribution to the development of the Argentine capital markets by cooperating with the Central Bank's efforts to standardize mortgage loan contracts so that, in the future, Collateral Mortgage Obligations (CMOs) could be traded more efficiently;
- Many important downstream effects on building products, furniture, household appliances, and consumer goods resulting from the acceleration of housing construction;
- Development of new infrastructure (roads, schools, etc.) connected to the new residential areas; and
- Generation of additional government tax revenues (more than US$2 million annually).

Initial Estimates of Developmental Effects

At the time MIGA issued its guarantee, it was expected that substantial positive development effects would arise from the investment. Clearly, the program would provide urgently needed affordable, long-term mortgage financing, and it would help relieve the deficit in Argentina's housing stock. Since 1960, residential mortgage loans were rare, and the maximum tenor was only five years. The short amortization period, coupled with high interest rates (about 20 percent per year), led to onerous repayment terms. Consequently, mortgages were costly and available only to the highest income earners.

It was estimated at the time that the proposed loan would allow Banco de Boston to offer 10-year maturities, thereby doubling amortization periods and lowering mortgage payments; this would significantly expand the number of qualifying applicants from lower income levels. It was also expected that the availability of additional

– 51 –

funding for mortgages would stimulate various sectors of the construction and home furnishing industries, resulting in increased employment.

It was anticipated that the program would add 40 new jobs at Banco de Boston. Extensive training was planned, since so few long-term mortgages had been written in Argentina, and local experience in writing such mortgages was nearly nonexistent. BankBoston planned to send a team of experienced mortgage bankers to Argentina to train staff at Banco de Boston, install a management information system, and inaugurate new administrative procedures.

In the long run, Banco de Boston planned to develop a full securitization program of mortgages in Argentina by converting mortgages into collateralized mortgage obligations (CMOs) to be sold both to domestic and overseas investors. With the US$50 million MIGA-guaranteed loan, Banco de Boston expected to engender an additional increase in the volume of mortgages by selling participation in them to investors. This plan was viewed at the time as an important step towards the development of the Argentine capital market. BankBoston was hoping to transfer its U.S. mortgage securitization skills to Argentina.

The national treasury was expected to benefit from the expansion. Banco de Boston estimated that it would pay the government of Argentina an additional US$1.9 million in taxes annually over the term of the loan.

Ex-Post Evaluation of Economic and Developmental Impacts

In April 1997, an independent consultant, retained by MIGA, visited Banco de Boston in Argentina and met with its managers and staff to gather information that would provide the basis to assess the developmental impact of the project. Banco de Boston was particularly cooperative with MIGA's efforts to evaluate the program's developmental impact. Managers and staff at the Buenos Aires headquarters were very informative concerning the Banco de Boston's operations to date. They provided complete access to relevant documentation and also facilitated the project monitor's visit to a Banco de Boston housing project supported by the MIGA-assisted mortgage program.

Overall Assessment

The initiation of a mortgage program in Argentina was a bold step by BankBoston. It predicated its loan to Banco de Boston on the passage and success of the Convertibility Plan. In addition, MIGA assumed some risk in issuing its guarantee before the effects of the plan were clear and the government's determination to suppress inflation had been demonstrated. MIGA supported this investment in Argentina despite of the financial collapse of the National Mortgage Bank, the inability of the government to implement the IBRD's housing project, and the untested impacts of the Convertibility Plan. As it will be noted in the following sections, the risks assumed by BankBoston (and MIGA) in supporting this investment have yielded substantial developmental benefits for the Argentine economy.

The funds originally guaranteed by MIGA leveraged considerable private sector resources into the mortgage market in Argentina. The MIGA guarantee of

US$50 million allowed Banco de Boston to initially gain a significant percentage of the long-term mortgage market. The mortgage market grew exponentially.[27] As of the end of July 1997, this market had more than $4 billion in dollar-denominated mortgage loans and $3 billion in peso-denominated mortgage loans.[28]

The success of Banco de Boston's mortgage program was attributable to many factors. The most important was, of course, the government's adoption of, and its rigorous adherence to, its 1991 Convertibility Plan (mandating a one-to-one exchange rate with the U.S. dollar), which succeeded in stabilizing the country's economy by curbing inflation. Banco de Boston also benefited from its leadership position in the field of residential mortgages. In addition, however, MIGA's guarantee was a determinant factor in BankBoston's decision to invest in the program.

The Implementation of the Mortgage Program

The evaluation of this investment verified that this mortgage program was a great success, both for the investor and for Argentina. Banco de Boston initiated its mortgage program in June of 1992. By September 1992, when it wrote its first 10-year loans with the MIGA-insured funds, its portfolio of mortgage loans grew to reach US$29 million dollars. By January 1994, Banco de Boston's total portfolio of 10-year mortgages was US$53 million. In October 1993, in view of the early success of the program, Banco de Boston announced the start of its 20-year mortgage loans.

Banco de Boston's mortgage program was not only well received by potential customers, but also by the press that reported extensively about it. The media highlighted Banco de Boston's bold move to offer 20-year mortgage loans at reduced interest rates, and at the same time, eliminating the 3.5 percent "compensation charges."[29] Newspapers noted Banco de Boston's flexible eligibility criteria for credit. In 1993, it was reported that the income requirement of 1,500 pesos monthly was the lowest in the market at the time.[30] In 1997, the income requirements were even lower: US$1,200 dollars monthly for Buenos Aires and US$1,000 dollars monthly for the provinces.

As of April 1997, Banco de Boston had nearly 3,000 residential home mortgages for new homes in its portfolio, worth US$280 million, plus an additional 2,400 mortgages for home improvement. The mortgage lending was the bank's largest program, comprising about 55 percent of its noncommercial portfolio in 1997, or about 6.5

---

[27] The growth of the mortgage market is not attributable to asset inflation. Data provided by the Banco Hipotecario Nacional (BHN) showed that the average price in U.S. dollars of a housing square meter have remained relatively stable in recent years.

[28] Figures supplied by the Institute of Economic Studies, Universidad de la Empresa with data from the Banco Hipotecario Nacional (BHN).

[29] *Buenos Aires Herald*, Buenos Aires, Argentina, "Bank of Boston Cuts Mortgages Rates," December 22, 1993.

[30] *El Informador Publico*, Buenos Aires, Argentina, "Banco de Boston Sigue en la Pelea," interview of Manuel Sacerdote, President of Banco de Boston, Argentina, October 12, 1993, p. 14.

percent of its total assets. The mortgage program's impressive growth continued; the monthly average of issued mortgage loans increased from US$14 million in 1996 to $18 million as of April 1997.

Despite its vastly increased residential mortgage portfolio, as of December 1997, Banco de Boston had not yet found it necessary to initiate a securitization program by selling participation to foreign investors, as originally envisioned. In the meantime, other banks in the country began to bundle packages of their high-quality mortgages for sale to domestic and foreign interests, but since Banco de Boston had not yet reached its internal ceiling for hypothecation, they had not yet gone to the marketplace to raise additional funds. Banco de Boston was also adapting its mortgage loan contracts to a model promoted by the Argentine Central Bank with the objective of standardizing mortgage contracts. Standardization is a precondition for the development of a market where CMOs can be traded efficiently.

The Financial Sector

Banco de Boston maintained consistent leadership in the field of residential mortgages. In 1992, it was the first bank to offer 10-year terms, a precedent which other banks began to follow six months later, after they witnessed Banco de Boston's substantial success in the marketplace. Shortly after, in October 1993, it was also the first Bank to offer 20-year mortgage loans. The press at that time reported that by doing so Banco de Boston "set market standards and forced other banking institutions to adapt to its parameters."[31] In this regard, it was noted that this type of long-term loan had not been available in Argentina in 30 years. When this new product (20-year mortgage loan) was introduced, the longest terms in the market were being offered by *Banco de Galicia* (12 years) and *Banco Francés* (15 years).[32] This new product further spurred the competition among mortgage lenders.

The introduction of 10-year loans, followed by 20-year loans, had an important financial market impact. Figures 11 and 12 depict the development of Banco de Boston's portfolio composition. In August 1992, all loans had a maturity of five years. In April 1997, five-year loans constituted only about 25 percent of Banco de Boston's portfolio; but 58 percent of the portfolio is comprised of 10-year loans, and the bank had 17 percent of its mortgage portfolio in *20* year loans.

Another important financial market impact was the availability of lower mortgage interest rates in Argentina. Banco de Boston, in response to the vigorous competitive situation which has arisen since it inaugurated its program, was aggressive in reducing its interest rates, inducing other banks to follow its lead. In 1992, interest

---

[31] *Buenos Aires Herald*, Buenos Aires, Argentina, "Bank of Boston Cuts Mortgages Rates," December 22, 1993.

[32] *La Nación*. Buenos Aires, Argentina, "Vuelve el Largo Plazo en los Créditos para Vivienda," October 13, 1993.

Figure 11. Mortgage Terms, September 1992
(% of portfolio)

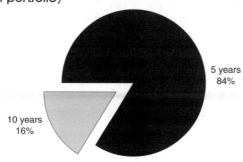

Figure 12. Mortgage Terms, April 1997
(% of portfolio)

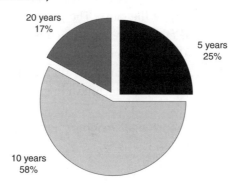

rates were between 19 and 22 percent (depending on the size of the loan) for mortgages up to 10 years. One year later, interest rates went down to between 15 and 17 percent for mortgages up to 20 years.

In 1997, Banco de Boston was charging between 12 and 15 percent interest for mortgages, the exact amount dependent upon whether the loan is denominated in dollars or carries a floating peso rate. At the time the monitoring trip took place, this interest rate was likely to continue to decrease in the next year or two. In any event, these rates represented a substantial improvement for the prospective homeowner over the 23 percent rate of interest that prevailed on short-term mortgages at the time MIGA originally issued its guarantee. Obviously, this competitive situation brought substantial savings to consumers.

Direct Employment Effect

Banco de Boston officers estimated that there were about 200 employees working directly on the new mortgage program in 1997 (compared to the projected 40 new employees that the bank was originally planning to hire for the program). These employees worked in sales, marketing, credit analysis and administration of the program. There were many more new employees if one took into account other support functions in the Bank such as accounting, and management information systems. Mortgage lending became such a profit center for the bank that plans were under way to open an additional 130 branches throughout Argentina. In 1997, there were about eight branch operations in the provinces outside of Buenos Aires, and plans called for expanding this number to about 80. This would result in an additional 400 people being added to Banco de Boston's staff—not all of them, of course, to handle the mortgage program, but that program underlined the vast expansion being contemplated.

Investment in Human Capital

Banco de Boston representatives confirmed that the extensive training program detailed at the time when the MIGA guarantee was issued was carried out as described, and that training in various aspects of credit analysis as it pertains to residential financing was an ongoing activity of the bank. The program included training in financial statement analysis and evaluation, credit analysis, and credit proposals, and provides an overview of the bank's policies, strategies, services, and operations. Trainees in the Credit Administration Department attend courses in international banking, investment banking, finance, and technical English.

Figure 13. Banco de Boston Mortgage Program, Employment Generation

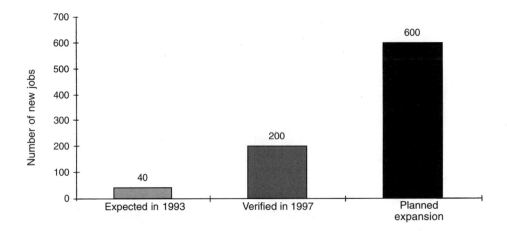

Increased Access to Housing

The combination of longer terms and lower interest rates unleashed the pent-up demand for housing, as home ownership has become a financially viable alternative to renting. Although no hard statistics were available at the time of the project evaluation, Banco de Boston staff estimated that about 70 percent of its mortgage funds went to middle- and upper-middle-class families (i.e., people earning between 30,000 and 80,000 pesos per year) who previously had been compelled to rent or save for a very long time (or get money from their employer or family) to own a house. Moreover, Banco de Boston was progressively lowering its minimum income requirement to qualify for its mortgage loans; the requirements of US$1,200 dollars for applicants from Buenos Aires and US$1,000 dollars monthly for applicants from the interior provinces made it accessible to many more middle-class customers throughout the country. This mortgage program undoubtedly improved the living conditions of many Argentineans.

Upstream and Downstream Effects

The increasing availability of home mortgages became one of the important forces driving the Argentine economy. The recession after the Mexican crisis forced Argentina's government to reexamine its development priorities, focusing on developing the construction sector to further stimulate economic activity and reduce unemployment.[33] As a result of this project evaluation exercise, it was verified that in early 1997 the cement industry in the country had almost reached its capacity,[34] and the steel industry, which supplied about 40 percent of its output to construction-related projects, had experienced a 40 percent increase in annual demand from the construction sector. In addition, the production of iron for construction uses had increased by an impressive 107 percent between 1991 and 1997.

Provision of new housing was also in consonance with one of the government's objectives to reduce an unemployment rate that hovered around 16 percent. Affordable home mortgages increased the rate at which privately owned suburban houses and condominiums were built. In addition, householders started major improvement projects when purchasing apartments in existing buildings. The growth in construction of new homes also spurred the sale of home appliances with the associated effects on employment and technology improvement. New houses require better and more technologically advanced products.

Demonstration Effect

The success of its operations in Argentina, including the residential mortgage program, prompted BankBoston's follow-up investment decisions. In September 1997, the *Financial Times*[35] reported that BankBoston has agreed to acquire Deutsche Bank Argentina for US$250 million cash in a "move to strengthen its large retail franchise in Latin America." The report added that this acquisition followed BankBoston's recently announced plans to add 70 new branches in Argentina, primarily in the interior provinces. It was also noted that Mr. Henrique Meirelles, BankBoston's Head of Latin American operations, met with President Menem to garner his support. Mr. Meirelles expressed his intentions to "make operations in the region [Latin America] a cornerstone of BankBoston's global strategy."

---

[33] In the period 1990–96 the construction sector grew by 70 percent in real terms, becoming one of the most dynamic economic activities in Argentina.

[34] This is following an impressive growth in the period 1991–97 of 45 percent in the delivery of cement in the domestic market. (Source: Institute for Economic Studies–Universidad Argentina de la Empresa (UADE) with data from the Asociación de Fabricantes de Cemento Portland.)

[35] *Financial Times*, "BankBoston in $250m Argentine buy," Companies and Finance: The America, September 30, 1997, p. 24.

A Related Project Site Visit

In the context of the monitoring trip, MIGA was advised of a housing project connected to the Banco de Boston's mortgage program. The consultant visited a precedent-setting suburban residential community located within half an hour commute of Buenos Aires. *Campos de Echeverria*, as it is known, is a community which will contain 214 well-constructed and attractive middle-class homes. Good schools for children as well as access to adequate shopping facilities are available. Banco de Boston's role in the project was substantial. It supplied the construction financing for the development and, as an added benefit, was aggressively providing the individual mortgages involved. Once again, witnessing the early success of this project, other banks in the country have begun to follow suit, so that one could expect a substantial increase in these kinds of housing developments over the following years.

The importance of *Campos de Echeverria* was that by utilizing economies of scale, in terms of architectural and construction services, the project developers were able to offer housing units to an element of the population that heretofore could not afford it. The developers targeted a market segment of young families with incomes in a range between 30,000 and 70,000 pesos annually, which put them in the country's middle class. (The houses in the community were priced from 95,000 to 115,000 pesos.)

Conclusion

The impact on improving the quality of life of many Argentineans is clearly evident. After decades of housing shortages and an acute lack of long-term credit, the program initiated by the Banco de Boston provided many Argentineans with the opportunity to own their own home. The accessibility of mortgage loans offered the hope of ownership to many middle-class Argentineans who did not have it previously, given the prevailing onerous loan terms.

The other positive aspects of the project were substantial; it has and will continue to make an important contribution to Argentina's economic development. Residential housing is likely to continue to be a significant component of the construction sector, which in turn has become one of the country's leading economic stimulants and an important employment generator. In addition, there has been a substantial multiplier effect on businesses throughout Argentina resulting from the acceleration of housing construction and the resultant indirect employment generation. Banco de Boston found a new and profitable line of business which supported a substantial expansion of its operations in the country as a whole, and created increased employment opportunities in the bank. Indeed, Argentina's banking sector as a whole benefited from the Banco de Boston's precedent-setting initiative; this program stimulated the banking activities of other institutions by fostering innovative financial products and increasing employment opportunities throughout the financial sector.

In sum, MIGA's relatively small, but timely, intervention had a beneficial effect on Argentina's economic and social development in the mid-1990s. Moreover, BankBoston's expansion plans in Argentina and its investment in housing development were indications that the positive impacts of this investment would continue into the future.

C. Crescent Greenwood, Ltd., Pakistan[36]

Introduction

The primary purpose of this paper is to report the developmental impacts of the Crescent Greenwood, Ltd., project in Pakistan. This project exemplifies how several institutions within the World Bank Group cooperatively worked to establish a framework in which the project could be undertaken and describes the role that political risk insurance played in this joint effort. Even though the report is not intended to portray all of the project's effects on Pakistan's economic development, a brief overview of the country's current economic situation and the World Bank's strategic objectives is included. A summary description of Pakistan's important textile sector is portrayed to provide an appropriate background.

The current status of the project and its developmental impacts will be examined, especially those pertaining to employment creation and creating job opportunities for women. The company's introduction of important new technology into the country and the comprehensive training of its workforce to properly manage the new equipment will be reviewed. The upstream and downstream effects of the project will be evaluated as well as the project's impact on the country's economy. A section is devoted to environmental and worker safety issues.

Project Background

In fiscal 1993, MIGA issued a contract of guarantee of US$8.4 million to Greenwood Mills, a U.S. company located in the state of South Carolina, for its US$9.85 million investment in the construction and operation of a fully integrated garment production facility in Pakistan. Thereafter, because some additional expected investment from other investors failed to materialize, Greenwood Mills increased its investment to US$13.8 million, of which MIGA later agreed, in fiscal 1995, to cover a total of US$12.0 million. MIGA insured Greenwood Mills against the risks of Currency Transfer Restriction, Expropriation and War and Civil Disturbance.

Greenwood Mills is a privately held U.S. textile manufacturing corporation whose primary business is the production of denim garments which are sold to major apparel manufacturers (such as Levis Strauss) in the U.S. and Europe. At the time the guarantee was issued, it operated 18 production facilities in the U.S. and one abroad, employing approximately 7,200 people. Its partner in the project, Crescent Textile Mills, is the flagship company of the Crescent Group, an extremely large and highly diversified textile, manufacturing, and service organization in Pakistan. The group owns a number of textile mills, jute and sugar production facilities, paper and paper product companies, steel mills, and insurance, leasing, bulk storage and banking firms.

---

[36] This report is a revised version of a project evaluation report prepared in July 1997 by Mr. Michael R. Stack, an independent consultant retained by MIGA's Guarantees Department. His activities, including a two-day visit to the project site in Pakistan, were coordinated by Mr. Gerald T. West and Ms. Ethel I. Tarazona of the Guarantees Department.

– 59 –

Majority stockholders in the joint venture company are Crescent Textile Mills and Greenwood Mills. The IFC and the Asian Finance and Investment Corporation, Ltd. (AFIC), are minority investors. The project involved the construction and operation of a greenfield project, Crescent Greenwood, Ltd., in Punjab at a rural site about half way between Lahore and Faisalabad. The project consisted in a fully integrated denim garment mill to spin, weave, finish, cut, wash, dry, and sew fine quality denim five pocket jeans for export, primarily to Europe. It also included a dedicated power plant and water purification facility. It was anticipated that with 60 looms the project could produce about 8 million pairs of jeans annually. The investor estimated that the project would employ some 400 people during the construction phase and create about 2,800 permanent jobs. Training was to be provided for management by Greenwood Mills, and sewing know-how by Feldon House, a British company.

The availability of political risk insurance was critical to the foreign investor. Greenwood Mills had sought a guarantee from the Overseas Private Investment Corporation (OPIC) in connection with the transaction but was turned down because the corporation was off-cover at the time by reason of U.S. law. Greenwood Mills then applied successfully to MIGA for assistance. The importance of MIGA's assistance was confirmed in a letter by the company's Executive Vice President for Finance:

> Greenwood Mills' participation in the Crescent Greenwood Project in Pakistan represents a sizable investment for our Company in a foreign country. Greenwood deliberated long and hard before making this investment and decided to go ahead with their commitment once we were able to purchase Political Risk insurance through Multilateral Investment Guarantee Agency.

> Because this insurance was available to Greenwood Mills and covered us for expropriation, currency transfer, and war and civil disturbance, we were able to justify our investment in a developing Third World country. However, the Project in Pakistan has been received well by the Pakistani government and the Pakistani people.

> Without this insurance coverage by MIGA, we would have been very hesitant to make this type of commitment for such a venture. The people at MIGA have been most helpful in helping us select the type of coverage for this type of risk and in advising us what is available. Their help and support is greatly appreciated.[37]

Economic Background[38]

Pakistan's economic performance over the past two decades has been characterized by rapid improvements in the growth of the country's GDP, led by the agricultural sector and cotton-based manufacturing. The increased growth rate can also be attributed to the stimulus provided by the country's highly enterprising private sector. As

---

[37] Letter from Paul E. Welder, Executive Vice President, Finance, to Michael Stack, October 28, 1997.
[38] The material in this section is a synopsis of a recent report by the World Bank Group published on the world wide web at http://www.worldbank.org/html/extdr/offrep/sas/p.htm entitled Pakistan, Social Profile, June 12, 1997.

a result, in that 20-year period per capita income climbed in real terms by more than 70 percent to about US$490 in 1996, and the percentage of the country's poor below the poverty line concomitantly declined from almost one-half to about one-third. Unfortunately, even though substantial progress has also been made in terms of human development, the country's social indicators remain low. Thus, for instance, while adult literacy increased by about 46 percent during those years, accompanied by some fairly significant percentage increases in enrollment in primary and in secondary education (especially among young females), Pakistan's overall school enrollment rates (of 46 percent for primary and 21 percent for secondary) are still only half the average for all low-income countries.

The country also suffers from pronounced gender disparities: Pakistan's female indicators compare unfavorably with both the averages for South Asia and low-income countries as a group. Only 21 percent of females over 15 years of age are literate, and only 31 percent of girls attend primary school. A major World Bank Country study, entitled "Women in Pakistan—an Economic and Social Strategy" (Pub. 8009), dated December 1989, which is still relevant, concluded that, "a major obstacle to Pakistan's transformation into a dynamic, middle-income economy is underinvestment in its people, particularly women."

With regard to the country's environment, poor natural resource management and a very high population growth rate have resulted in environmental degradation and pollution, adversely affecting public health and GDP growth. Water and wind erosion, salinization, waterlogging, and overgrazing have degraded about 42 percent of the land. Almost all surface water is contaminated by pollution from household and industrial waste water and agricultural runoff. Air pollution levels are rising and are especially severe in the two main cities of Karachi and Lahore.

Market Conditions: The Textile Sector

Cotton and cotton-based manufacturing account for two-thirds of Pakistan's exports. Recently some diversification within the sector has occurred, and the shipment of raw cotton and low-count yarn for processing abroad is slowly being replaced by the export of processed cotton, textiles, and garments. The overall share of *all* nontraditional merchandise, including these cotton-based goods, has more than tripled during the last decade. Thus, it is evident that the country's overall profile of exports is gradually undergoing profound changes. However, Pakistan must confront intense competition from other developing nations in Asia, many of which produce the same kinds of goods (including, of course, textiles and garments) for export. Consequently, the overall rate of export growth declined recently, which is essentially ascribed to increased international competition exacerbated by the country's failure to enact trade reforms and lower import tariffs to standardize it with the trade practices prevailing in other countries in the region.[39]

Nonetheless, the textile industry remains the most important manufacturing sector in Pakistan (the country is one of the world's top producers of cotton), accounting

---

[39] See http://www.worldbank.org/html/extdr/offrep/sas/p.htm–, pp. 34.

for an average of 40 percent of manufacturing employment, 62 percent of manufacturing exports, and 30 percent of manufacturing value added. The industry produces cotton yarn, cotton cloth, made-up textiles, and apparel. Despite recent efforts, such as the Crescent Greenwood project, to introduce high-tech equipment, the industry still is mired in the preliminary stages of textile processing. In general, large firms concentrate on spinning and weaving, leaving garment-making to highly fragmented small to medium-sized producers. Many observers believe that Pakistan's textile industry urgently needs to rationalize its operations and make the move to higher value-added production to respond to the challenges and opportunities afforded by the phased elimination of quotas under the Uruguay Round trade agreement. Otherwise, it will be greatly disadvantaged in its efforts to keep pace with very aggressive and well-organized competitors in Asia.

Complementarity with the World Bank Group

Since the election of Nawaz Sharif as Prime Minister, economic and fiscal policy making have improved considerably. A "supply-side" budget has been adopted which significantly reduces the rate of taxation on both individuals and businesses. To compensate for lost revenue, the government is attempting to increase significantly the tax base so that more than the current 900,000 Pakistanis (out of a population of 130 million) pay taxes, essentially by reducing tax rates and broadening the tax base to include hitherto untaxed income and undertaxed sectors, supported by improvements in tax administration. Just as importantly, a major trade policy reform, actually reducing import tariffs, has been carried out, which is expected to serve as a powerful incentive to the business community.

To ensure the success of these new programs and the continued progress of reform efforts, all members of the bank group need to cooperate in carrying out their programs. Clearly, the Crescent Greenwood project exemplifies this cooperation. The IBRD/IDA has had a long-standing and ongoing policy dialog with Pakistan over measures to enable the private sector to achieve sustained rapid growth on the basis of higher productivity and enhanced international competitiveness, as well as diversification of production and exports. The company from the outset has clearly benefited from these policy discussions which over the years have covered matters crucial to export-oriented firms. These include trade reform, with the explicit objective of removing a variety of anti-export biases; comprehensive reform of the banking system, for instance, to strengthen the capacity of the Central Bank to engage in prudent regulation and supervision; and agricultural reforms, which goes to the heart of their business—purchasing high-quality, reasonably priced cotton from farmers.

Moreover, the IFC played a fundamental role in this project. The IFC is the senior lender to the project and incurs substantial risk as a shareholder. The Corporation's equity stake in the project was vital to Greenwood Mills' decision to join Pakistan's Crescent Group in the venture. IFC also played an important advisory role in project design, and its participation helped to ensure that AFIC would also become involved in the enterprise. The IFC's input was especially critical in the environmental and worker safety areas, insisting that World Bank criteria and standards be applied from project inception. (MIGA relied on the IFC's environmental expertise to ensure there were no problems in this area at the time the Agency approved its guarantee for the project.)

Box 7. Development Highlights: Crescent Greenwood, Pakistan

- Employment of about 2,750 individuals, of whom about 13 percent are women, with good working conditions, benefits, and training programs.
- An annual expenditure of close to US$20 million in 1996, the first full year of operations, for local inputs, principally cotton, but also for locally sourced equipment and spare parts.
- Benefits to businesses involved in providing transportation and employment services.
- Use of state-of-the-art equipment.
- The project's success has demonstrated to the international business community the feasibility of producing high-quality consumer merchandise at a competitive price.
- Generation of US$19.2 million in export earnings in 1996 and payment of US$3.2 million in duties and taxes to the government.
- Provision of housing, schooling for dependents (and others in the surrounding community), transportation, medical services, and recreation facilities for employees.
- Careful attention is paid to environmental practices and worker safety to ensure responsible corporate management of these issues.

Ex-Post Evaluation of Economic and Developmental Impacts

On June 30 and July 1, 1997, the independent project evaluation consultant to MIGA visited the premises of the production facility and the company's Lahore headquarters. In both locations he met with company managers and staff to gather information for an assessment of the impact of the project. The consultant had been previously briefed on the project and the type of information needed for this analysis by MIGA Guarantee staff members in Washington, D.C., who also provided him with full access to the Agency's project file as background.

Crescent Greenwood's managers and staff members (and Greenwood Mills, MIGA's client) were exceptionally cooperative with the Agency's effort to evaluate the project's developmental impact. Full briefings were provided by company personnel on every stage of the production process and aspect of the operation, with special emphasis on the project's environmental elements, and provided unstinting access to the project site and company employees. As a result of this visit, the company completed the MIGA detailed project questionnaire and provided MIGA with additional information on the financial, technical, environmental, and staff development aspects of the project. This report is based primarily on that information as well as the observations of the independent project monitor. The Resident Mission in Islamabad, which includes the original IFC project loan officer on its staff, was also consulted.

The project began commercial production in June 1995, and now occupies a 450-acre site near the small village of Bahuman in the vicinity of Faisalabad. The plant is divided into two distinct operations. The first part of the process (which is carried out around the clock all year long) consists of turning raw cotton into thread, then dyeing it and converting it into denim fabric. The final stage of this part of the fabrication process is using computer-assisted equipment to cut the cloth into the 18 components of a typical pair of blue jeans. The design of each of these sections is distinctive, and based on precise specifications provided by the European and American brand-name purveyors who purchase merchandise from the factory. The fabrication process is, then, largely mechanical in nature: generally speaking, the task of the all-male workforce is to tend the machines and keep the premises clean, transport goods through the production process, and inspect and pack finished garments for shipment abroad.

The second part of the operation, and by far the most labor-intensive aspect of the entire project, is assembling and stitching of the various pieces of precut material to make a finished pair of jeans—and then doing some of the final quality checks preparatory to packing and sending the goods to the purchaser. This sewing operation is located in a separate building away from the main factory and primarily employs women in the process. The women work only two shifts (never late-night/early morning). The work is extremely specialized, each woman repeating a particular part of the assembly process many times over during the course of the working day. It is evident that the work is highly skilled and precise in nature. Thus, it is in this part of the operation in which the concern for quality is primary, since, as noted above, the production of the fabric is automated and its quality, therefore, basically assured.

Economic Effect

Because of start-up problems encountered by the company, at the time of the evaluation, the project was unable to provide the substantial economic benefits originally estimated. Crescent Greenwood expected that it would average about US$53 million in exports each year, whereas in fact its exports were valued at only about US$19 million in 1996. Projections for calendar year 1998, however, anticipate about US$60 million in exports, based on the flow of orders and the securing of the ISO certificate. Accordingly, in the near future, taking into account the many changes and improvements which have occurred, the company may well be poised to exceed its original expectations.

The company was also burdened by higher duties imposed on it than was originally anticipated, because expected reduction in rates did not take place as promised by the former regime. Initial estimates foresaw paying taxes and duties of about US$1.2 million annually. In 1996, the project enterprise actually paid about three times that amount—around US$3.2 million. Because of the reduction of import tariffs mentioned previously, and completion of import equipment requirements, in 1998 the company expected to pay less than the US$1.2 million originally foreseen.

In 1996 Crescent Greenwood also expended much less than the US$17 million in imported goods and services it thought it would have to procure annually. As a result of a general belt-tightening, in order to help obtain additional external financing, the company only purchased about US$6 million, cutting back foreign consultants and deferring other expenses for imported nonessential goods and services. That same year, the company did not remit any dividends to its owners. It was, however, obliged to make interest payments of about US$3.2 million to the IFC and others, which is considerably more than it expected (the company only anticipated having to make about US$2.2 million of total interest and dividend payments).

Investment in Human Capital

To assure prospective buyers that high-quality clothing was produced by the new operation, which is located in a country not previously known for turning out designer apparel, the company embarked on a vigorous—and ultimately successful—campaign to obtain ISO (International Standards Organization, headquartered in Switzerland) certification. To meet the rigorous quality standards imposed by the ISO, the company undertook a comprehensive review of all aspects of its operations, and then engaged in an extensive training program for *all* employees on the details of ISO's multiple requirements. The intensive training program, which spanned more than a year, was rewarded when, on August 11, 1997, after a two-day audit of plant operations, the company was granted an ISO 9002 certificate.

Moreover, the company undertook extensive training of its employees. In addition to the intensive ISO training discussed above, Crescent Greenwood sponsored on-premises classes in development of computer skills, and sent relevant personnel to both Karachi and Lahore for courses in marketing and management. Key members of the accounting department as well as department heads of the several major technical divisions were sent to Greenwood Mills plants in South Carolina for on-the-job training.

Direct Employment Effect

As expected, the company employed about 400 workers during the project's construction phase. At the time of the visit, it employed just under 2,750 workers on a permanent basis (about the number estimated in its application to MIGA). However, revisions in Greenwood's personnel structure were significantly more favorable than originally anticipated. In its Definitive Application for a guarantee, the company forecast that it would have 121 managers, 75 professional/technical employees, and 2,553 unskilled/semiskilled workers. There were to be no expatriates employed at the facility. In practice, however, the company reported that 72 of its employees were in management, 1,546 (including four expatriates) were placed in the professional/technical category, and 1,132 were categorized as unskilled/semiskilled workers. This revision in the personnel structure had important implications for the company's salary structure, as discussed below; and was in part attributable to the fact that the company, contrary to what was expected at the time of its MIGA Application, was not farming out its sewing operation to subcontractors.

– 65 –

Environmental Effects

Crescent Greenwood clearly demonstrated its intention to take on a beneficial environmental leadership role in the country. For example, while not under any legal obligation to do so, the company planted 200,000 trees on 78 acres of its 450 acre site. This afforestation effort extended outside the plant compound as well—21 acres of eucalyptus have been planted elsewhere in the nearby community. As noted in one of its reports, this effort had a "pleasant effect on the climate as a whole. By so much greenery, we have [succeeded in reducing] the hardships of the summer season and its related suffocation."

Protecting Pakistan's environment is an abiding concern of company management, and it is clear that a great deal of money was spent; continual, diligent efforts have been devoted to ensure that neither the atmosphere nor the land suffers from the effects of the various manufacturing processes. A local environmental council and Pakistan's environmental protection agency (which has issued a formal commendation to the company for its exemplary efforts) continually monitor plant operations. Since the facility was initially designed to conform to World Bank standards, very few problems have arisen.

All smokestacks from the electrical generating plant and other chimneys in the facility are equipped with emission control devices. As a result, there were no visible emissions anywhere resulting from the mill's operations. Flue gases have not yet been measured, but the company has been assured by the manufacturers of the generating plant and other equipment that they have been designed to meet rigorous environmental standards. Nonetheless, measuring equipment was being imported by the company, and the appropriate *in situ* tests were to be performed by a skilled consultant firm and confirmed by government scientists.

With regard to liquid effluent, the large waste water treatment plant on the premises separated the considerable amount of water used in the dyeing process from the sludge which remains, consisting entirely of indigo and sizing (a kind of starch). The intention of the company is to purify the wastewater to an extent which would enable it to be used for agricultural irrigation. To date, this standard was not yet achieved because chemicals used in the purification process rendered the water too saline. However, experts diagnosed the problem and recommended a specific change in the composition of the chemicals used. After these recommended chemicals are obtained and utilized, it is expected that the problem will be entirely resolved, and farmers can then be given access to the water. It should be added that the plant's wastewater was regularly tested, in a fully equipped, on-premise laboratory, to assure that it contained no harmful microorganisms or dangerous chemicals.

Similarly, the disposal of sludge is under investigation. At present, it is simply removed from the waste disposal facility and buried in unlined pits outside the plant's premises. Company management represented that there are no heavy metals or other poisons in this waste product which could seep into the water table supplying the surrounding villages. Crescent Greenwood's proposal was to convert this sludge to fertilizer by mixing it with molasses; the company was testing the feasibility of this process.

In addition, it is important to stress that the ISO certificate not only imposes rigorous quality requirements, but also details the processes to be utilized to ensure that goods are produced in a responsible and appropriate manner. Thus, the standards cover such issues as child labor, environmental considerations, safe working conditions, fire drill procedures, etc.

Poverty Alleviation and Workers' Benefits

As noted previously, Pakistan's per capita GDP is the rupee equivalent of approximately US$460 per annum. Currently, the minimum wage in the country is established by law at US$585 per year. Most of the company's employees in the fabrication plant earn more than this figure, on average about US$750 yearly. Many of these people fall into the unskilled/semiskilled labor category.

About 1,600 of the workers live on-site (there are both bachelor and family quarters) and about 350 of the company's employees are women, who commute via company buses each day from nearby villages to the plant. Working conditions are generally good. All employees receive 30 days of paid leave yearly which includes vacation time, medical and emergency leave. There are, moreover, fourteen official holidays in the country which are also provided to the workers (employees receive overtime pay for working on these holidays). There is a company cafeteria, a 24-hour infirmary staffed by a nurse and, three hours a day, by a physician, and an on-premises prayer room. The company has its own fully equipped fire department at the plant site. All workers put in an eight-hour, six-day per week schedule in accordance with Pakistan's labor code. No serious injuries have been reported during plant operations.

Social Development

Opportunities for Women

The average annual wage of the seamstresses (who fall within the "professional/technical" category) was approximately US$1,440, almost double that which the male employees on average earn in the fabric production facility. Wages constituted only a part of this sum: the women's base salaries were significantly bolstered by both productivity and quality incentives. This level of income for young women was a remarkable achievement in rural Pakistan. As Michael Essex, the IFC representative in the country has noted, "The social impact and empowerment of these women who for the first time are prime income earners in their family is significant and precedent setting."

Crescent Greenwood also had a policy of internal promotion. One woman (out of 72 employees in the "management" category) had benefited substantially from this arrangement. The head of the Customer Quality Assurance Department, an important position in the factory, was a woman promoted through the ranks after starting on the sewing room floor. There were, in addition, a number of female supervisors in the sewing facility, who, while not included in the category of top management, nonetheless held responsible positions in the organization—and all of whom were also promoted from within the ranks of seamstresses. The reason, however, that there were not more women in management roles stems from the value system of an extremely traditional society in which women are expected to marry at a relatively early age, and quickly thereafter become housewives and mothers. They generally do not stay employed long enough to acquire the seniority and experience needed for executive positions within a company.

Crescent Greenwood Public School

This facility deserves separate mention, because it best symbolized the company's aspirations to good corporate citizenship. An attractive schoolhouse and playground was located on the company's property, situated next to the main road so that it was easily accessible to the surrounding community. It provided classes from nursery school to the 10th year of education, and was not only available to the children of employees of the company, but to any child who desired to attend. There were 325 students, 215 male and 110 female; 182 of the students were from the surrounding community, and the rest were children of company employees. The staff of 21 teachers included the principal and 14 women. All hold university degrees, and five have their master's degree.

To facilitate and encourage attendance, the company subsidizes the tuition of poor students. Thus, a child from a poor farm family might only be charged as little as the equivalent of US$1.00 to attend for a semester. Given Pakistan's high rate of population growth, and the high quality of the education proffered by the school, it was expected that many more local children would attend the facility. Unhappily, such was not the case. Rural Pakistanis often expect their children to begin working and contributing to family income from about the age of five and help with chores on the family farm. This is especially true of young girls (the ratio of female to male students mentioned above is unusually high).

The company, nevertheless, remained optimistic about attracting additional students, reporting:

> As we are situated in a remote area and not much educational facilities are provided by the government, the community is looking forward for more educational facilities from us and Crescent Greenwood Public School is a symbol of hope for them. In the future we want to construct a large educational complex which will provide education until higher secondary school. This complex will enhance educational and vocational training facilities to the large part of the community of this area.[40]

If the company realizes this ambitious undertaking, and maintains the present high ratio of women teachers, it may, at least in its own region, contribute to resolving a part of the country's educational problem, particularly as it pertains to young girls:

---

[40] Previous citation was taken from a memorandum written by Michael Essex, IFC's country representative.

Lack of facilities for girls' education [is] now probably the binding constraint in most areas…. Increasingly, girls' education is seen as important, but there are not enough of the *right kind* of schools to meet parental demand. If the school is relatively close, and has a female teacher and facilities for drinking water and sanitation, then parents are more likely to send their daughters, at least up to the primary level.[41] *(emphasis in text)*

Other Social Development Effects

Because of its isolation, Crescent Greenwood created a comprehensive social and physical infrastructure to attract and retain employees. The initiation of a large, modern industrial enterprise in the midst of what was hitherto an impoverished and remote rural environment brought about the beginnings of some significant economic change in the region, benefiting both the company's personnel as well as members of the surrounding community. Broadly, some of these improvements were as follows:

- *Housing:* Employees and their families live in an impressive residential complex consisting of three hostels each containing 62 dormitories for bachelor employees; 88 single rooms for officers, and 262 housing units for employees with families. These living accommodations contrast sharply with traditional housing in the villages in the area; they are well designed and maintained, with modern sanitary facilities.

- *Transportation:* The company hired a fleet of six local buses to provide transportation to workers who choose to live in their villages in the region. As noted previously, few women elect to live in company quarters; most are transported daily to and from their homes in the surrounding area. Employment at the company is deemed so desirable that people commute from villages as far as 60 km from the factory.

- *Medical:* Basic medical care is provided to employees and their families. An infirmary on the premises is staffed around the clock by a nurse, and for three hours each day by a medical doctor. In addition, the company stated in the MIGA Project Monitoring Questionnaire that "a local government sponsored social security hospital which was dysfunctional has recommenced its service because of the project."

- *Recreation:* The company initiated the Crescent Greenwood Recreation Club which "has been constituted to involve each and every employee. The purpose of this club is to provide a healthy environment to work in." Two playing fields for cricket, football, hockey, and volleyball tournaments are situated adjacent to the factory, and, we are informed, there is keen interdepartmental rivalry in badminton under way. This program is supported by company and employee contributions.

---

[41] Idem.

Upstream and Downstream Effects

Upstream effects were significant. The company estimated that from operational start-up about two years ago, it procured locally produced goods and services valued at approximately US$26.5 million. These funds were paid to local suppliers of various store goods and spare parts items, as well as, of course, cotton merchants and vendors of other kinds of goods (e.g., lubricants) needed for the production process. Jobs have been created with transportation firms (not only of factory employees but of materials as well, i.e., trucking companies to transport imported production inputs from Karachi (such as dyestuffs), and the company's output of finished goods to that city for shipment abroad).

In terms of downstream effects, indirect employment was generated by companies which were hired to find and procure suitably qualified laborers and technicians, and firms that furnished services to the live-in staff, such as vendors of food and general groceries and other consumables such as clothing and toiletries, etc. Presumably, this effect also included the creation or expansion of microenterprises such as barber shops, cleaners, and other small retail operations, such as local banks. Finally, jobs were created as a result of the company's efforts to upgrade services in the village of Bahuman, in whose district it is located. Crescent Greenwood was engaged in an effort to improve the roadways, sanitation, potable water supply, and lighting of the little community. The company estimates that some 500 indirect jobs have been created as a result of the mill's establishment.

Demonstration Effect

The Crescent Greenwood project helped to enhance Pakistan's image in terms of providing an acceptable foreign direct investment environment. As a result of the policy assistance provided by the IMF/IBRD, the more positive attitude of the present government toward the private sector, and the recent and much-welcomed beginnings of a reduction of tension with neighboring India, the country's overall investment climate and image had begun to improve. If this precedent-setting project finds its niche in the world marketplace and becomes as profitable as anticipated, it could become an important showcase for the government to help attract other, sophisticated manufacturing enterprises to the country. It has, at a minimum, clearly become an important prototype, heralding Pakistan's ability to produce quality fashion products for worldwide export, utilizing modern manufacturing techniques and equipment.

Conclusion

When the guarantee was issued in fiscal 1993, the Crescent Greenwood project was expected to have substantial, positive developmental impacts on the host country. This expectation has been fully realized, and in some respects exceeded, by Crescent Greenwood, which has demonstrated its strong determination to become an exemplary corporate citizen within Pakistan. Careful attention was paid by the company to issues of worker safety and environmental protection. Additionally, the company has provided significant and rewarding opportunities for a large staff of female employees—a significant achievement in a country the World Bank has characterized as suffering from severe "gender disparities." In terms of broad developmental benefits, the project is in the forefront of helping the country to move to higher value-added production, i.e., quality garment-making, beyond just spinning and weaving textiles, so that the nation can realize the substantial economic benefits associated with the production of fashionable clothing for high-end markets.

From a development standpoint, Crescent Greenwood can be considered a model project. It provides high wages and training in a number of modern skills to a large number of people who might otherwise be relegated to a life of hard, poorly rewarded and unremitting toil as traditional agriculturists. To its credit, the company's recent financial hardship has not detracted from its proactively pursuing that goal. It is clearly determined to become a good corporate citizen of its host country, as witnessed by the tree planting project and the "neighborhood" school it has established. The company made a real effort to treat its employees well and with dignity.

In terms of Pakistan's critically important textile sector, this IFC/MIGA-sponsored operation served to demonstrate that the country's industry need not relegate itself to the lower end of the production spectrum, but rather can produce quality products which can become highly competitive and accepted in the world marketplace. If progress continues to be made on the country's economic policy and political fronts, Crescent Greenwood could serve as a bellwether for substantial new and technologically advanced investment in Pakistan.

Conclusions

The evaluation results described in this report represent a significant first step for MIGA, even if that step is modest compared to practices of larger or older development institutions. MIGA is pleased that it now has empirical evidence, systematically gathered, that MIGA-assisted investors have positively promoted economic development. It is also gratifying to have evidence that investors' original estimates of their projects' prospective developmental impacts turned out to be underestimates of the actual effects.

MIGA believes that its approach to evaluating development effectiveness is appropriate, but acknowledges that its future evaluation efforts need to be both broadened and deepened. The challenge of "measuring" the multidimensional impacts of private sector investments on the development process will remain a continuing challenge. Notwithstanding significant conceptual limitations and analytical difficulties, the Agency believes that it has proposed a useful framework for analyzing those multidimensional impacts.

As previously noted, the relatively small number of mature projects allowed MIGA to evaluate a high proportion of this group of projects. On the other hand, the small number of projects in the sample (25) does not allow for making statistical inferences to the far larger population of projects in MIGA's portfolio. MIGA intends to evaluate a larger sample of its projects for this purpose. The three in-depth studies of MIGA-assisted projects proved to be very useful in illustrating the developmental impacts of such investments. (They also served as a basis to test the evaluation framework and to identify further information needs.)

MIGA accepted very early in its evaluation efforts that this would be an evolutionary process for the Agency. It was decided not to wait until the completion of this first monitoring round to incorporate improvements in the evaluation process. Rather, improvements have been made in real time (i.e., as soon as shortcomings and solutions are identified). On balance, this proved to be an excellent approach which MIGA intends to continue. The "feedback" benefits of having staff monitoring some of its projects have already proven worthwhile. In the meantime, MIGA will continue to make improvements in the evaluation process and Project Monitoring Questionnaire in order to adequately capture the developmental effects of a wide variety of private sector enterprises.

Annex: Projects Evaluated
(as of June 1998)

Host country	Guarantee holder	Project description	Monitoring date	Contract dates
Argentina	BankBoston, N.A.	Financing facility for residential mortgages	April 1997	June 1992
Argentina	Citibank, N.A.	Financing facility for privatized companies	April 1997	May 1993
Argentina	ING Bank	Multipurpose financing facility for Argentinean companies	December 1997	November 1992
Bangladesh	Marubeni and Chiyoda Corporations	Construction and operation of a fertilizer processing plant	September 1996	February 1991 October 1992
Brazil	ING Bank	Expansion of branch banking operations	April 1997	September 1993
Brazil	BankBoston, N.A.	Medium-term US$ financing for equipment purchase & leasing	December 1997	October 1993
Brazil	BankBoston, N.A.	Expansion of branch banking operations	December 1997	August 1993
China	American Home Products Corporation	Pharmaceutical manufacturing & marketing facility (Suzhou-Lederle)	June 1996	July 1993
Costa Rica	Bank of Nova Scotia and Conservation Tourism	Ecotourism and research facility (The Rain Forest Aerial Tram)	November 1996	November 1994
Indonesia	Komatsu Limited	Metal forging manufacturing plant	November 1997	June 1992
Kazakhstan	ABN AMRO, N.V.	Establishment of bank branch	Received questionnaire on December 1997	June 1994
Pakistan	Société Générale	Expansion of branch banking operations	June 1996	December 1991 February 1993
Pakistan	Greenwood Mills	Construction and operation of integrated denim facility	June 1997	February 1995
Pakistan	Bank of America	Expansion of branch banking operations	June 1997	March 1993
Pakistan	Motorola Development Corporation	Installation and operation of a cellular phone system	June 1997	August 1993 March 1994
Pakistan	Crédit Agricole Indosuez	Expansion of branch banking operations	June 1997	May 1992 August 1993
Pakistan	Citibank, N.A.	Expansion of branch banking operations	June 1997	March 1992
Perú	ING Bank/AFP Integra	Equity participation in private pension fund management company	December 1997	July 1994

(Continues on following page)

Host country	Guarantee holder	Project description	Monitoring date	Contract dates
Perú	Volvo Perú	Extension of customer financing services	December 1997	July 1995
Perú	Citibank, N.A./ AFP Profuturo	Equity participation in private pension fund management company	December 1997	September 1993
Saudi Arabia	Guardian Glass, S.A.	Construction and operation of float glass manufacturing facility	April 1997	August 1995
South Africa	Harsco Corporation/ MultiServ International, N.V.	Steel slag processing plant	May 1997	March 1995
Trinidad & Tobago	PCS Nitrogen, Inc./ Arcadian Partners	Privatization of fertilizer facility	May 1997	March 1994
Turkey	SAS Partners/ Gate Gourmet	Privatization of airline catering and airport restaurant facilities	November 1997	June 1991
Turkey	Citibank, N.A.	Privatization & export financing facility	November 1997	October 1991

Appendix:
MIGA'S Support of Financial Sector Projects and Their Contribution to the Development Process

I. Introduction

In September 1997, several board members raised both theoretical and practical questions about MIGA's support of financial sector investments in terms of the developmental benefits of financial versus nonfinancial projects. As a supplement to its own evaluation efforts, MIGA management decided it would be useful to have these issues addressed by an external consultant with expertise in this area. As a result, Dr. Dimitri Plionis[42] was contracted to prepare a report that was appended to a broader report on July 28, 1998, to MIGA's Board of Directors on the Agency's development effectiveness.

Drawing on that report by Dr. Plionis, this appendix seeks, in summary fashion, to put some of these theoretical questions in context, notes how MIGA's role in this sector complements World Bank Group efforts, and reviews a sample of nine MIGA-assisted financial sector projects in terms of five evaluation criteria. The appendix concludes with some observations about some of the distinct development effects of financial sector projects.

II. Theoretical Background

Starting with the first treatment in modern times of financial systems and economic development by Joseph Schumpeter in 1949, a series of papers on the subject have appeared in the economic literature in the last half-century. Initially, these papers were theoretical and abstract with little practical relevance. In the last 10 years, however, a series of empirical studies conducted in a variety of settings have confirmed the existence of a direct, strong, and positive relationship between financial system development and economic growth. This rela-

---

[42] Dr. Dimitri Plionis is a consultant in economic reform and foreign direct investment. For 22 years he served in the consulting department of Ernst & Young, where, as a partner, he directed a number of international consulting groups, including the International Finance Services Group and the International Finance and Investment Consulting Services Group. During his career, Dr. Plionis performed consulting services on more than 100 projects in over 50 countries in Latin America, Eastern Europe, the former Soviet Union, and Asia. Projects involved privatization services, enterprise restructuring, cross-border investment, and trade consulting. Dr. Plionis is currently Leader of the Corporate Services Consulting Practice of the Barents Group, a KPMG company.

tionship is manifested primarily through an increase in the rate of capital accumulation and through improvements in the efficiency with which economies use that capital due to the services of the financial system. These papers, however, measure growth and development largely by means of macroeconomic variables and do not provide any information on developmental impacts at the firm or consumer level. Therefore, they do not lend themselves to establishing quantitative relationships between specific financial service inputs and specific developmental effects which could be used to measure the developmental effects of financial services projects.

There seems to be a clear link, however, between the availability of long-term debt financing and the level of productivity of an economy. Also, growth rates seem to be correlated with the types and quality of the financial services provided. Some of the types of financial services that seem to have a particularly positive impact are those related to the development of capital markets and of contractual savings instruments.[43] These types of financial services are often the focus or direct result of foreign investment projects.

The importance of financial systems for developing countries is further accentuated in recent years because private capital flows into them have increased tremendously. Such flows have been increasingly channeled by banks and capital markets throughout the developing economies.

A review of the literature supports and amplifies the positive aspects of foreign direct investment in the financial sectors of developing countries. For example, foreign investments in the financial sector are credited as a factor in attracting foreign direct investment in other sectors and in retaining local capital that might otherwise have been exported.[44] However, a number of concerns are also raised. While some of these concerns are similar to those expressed about foreign direct investment in general (for example, fear of foreign domination) and seem to reflect past attitudes which are fast becoming unfashionable in today's competitive global environment, others seem to have some validity. An example of such concerns is the notion that under certain conditions, foreign financial investment may provide unfair competition to local institutions, or that it may facilitate foreign portfolio investment which has been known to potentially cause problems in domestic capital markets.[45]

---

[43] See, for example, Caprio, Gerard, Jr., and A. Demirgüç-Kunt. 1997. "The Role of Long-Term Finance: Theory and Evidence." Policy Research Working Paper 1746. World Bank, Policy Research Department. Washington, D.C..

[44] See, for example, Wachtel, P. ,1996. "Foreign Banking in Central European Economies in Transition." In K. Mitzei and J. Bonin, eds., *Creating Market Oriented Banking Sector for the Economies in Transition,* New York: Institute for East-West Studies.

[45] It should be noted that at least one prominent researcher in the field, Gerard Caprio, downplays such concerns, citing either lack of adequate evidence or the positive effect, on balance, of foreign direct investment in the financial sector.

III. Supporting Financial Sector Investments

A. MIGA's Objective

As previously noted, MIGA was created to encourage the flow of investments for productive purposes among member countries, and in particular to developing member countries, thus supplementing the activities of the International Bank for Reconstruction and Development, the International Finance Corporation, and other international development finance institutions.

MIGA achieves its objective by screening for and, as appropriate, providing political risk insurance to investments presented to it by eligible investors, and by engaging in complementary investment promotional activities. In carrying out this mandate, MIGA must satisfy itself that the supported investments are sound, contribute to the development of the host country, and are consistent with the declared development objectives, priorities, and laws of the host country (MIGA Convention, Article 12). To ensure such consistency, Article 15 of the Convention requires MIGA to obtain the host country's prior approval.[46]

To put MIGA's support of financial sector investments in the proper perspective and in light of the requirement for the agency's activities to complement those of IBRD and the IFC, it is necessary to briefly look at the programs of those two institutions of the World Bank Group in support of the financial sector in developing countries.

B. Complementarity with the World Bank Group

The existence of a strong, positive relationship between financial services, and economic growth and development is well accepted within the World Bank Group. For example, the 1989 World Development Report, noting the increasing reliance of developing countries on the private sector and market mechanisms, underlines the great importance of financial systems to the efficient operation of both.[47] The World Bank Group's role in promoting robust and balanced financial structures in developing countries is clear.

In recent years, the World Bank Group has placed greater importance on the financial sector as a foundation for the growth of the real economy. President Wolfensohn's address to the Hong Kong Annual Meeting on September 23, 1997,

---

[46] Operational Regulation 3.28 specifies that MIGA "may also rely on a statement by the host country as evidence that the Investment Project conforms to the laws, regulations, objectives and priorities." MIGA has a policy to always secure such a statement, but, in addition, it conducts its own analysis of developmental effects (see Operational Regulation 3.06).

[47] The 1989 World Development Report, though dated, is the most comprehensive compendium of findings, conclusions, and recommendations regarding policies and practices of the World Bank Group in the financial sector. It is still very much relevant for, and is applied to, contemporary issues and problems in the sector.

underscored the importance of financial sector development for growth (especially in light of recent events in the Asian financial markets) and linked it to the alleviation of poverty. On November 17, 1997, in a letter to the vice presidents, President Wolfensohn cited the financial sector as one of the "key pressure points for change—those that will have the *biggest developmental impact*" (emphasis added).[48] In a recent initiative, the IBRD has announced the formation of a Special Financial Operations Unit to provide additional resources to other Bank units and to selected countries suffering from financial sector crisis.

Therefore, the promotion of efficient financial systems is an important objective of IBRD assistance. The IBRD uses the entire range of instruments at its disposal (from structural adjustment loans to technical assistance loans) to support financial sector development. The IBRD is actively involved in designing, structuring and executing projects to promote efficient financial systems. Furthermore, the IBRD is involved at the macroeconomic or sectoral level rather than at the level of individual financial institutions.

The IFC, on the other hand, supports individual equity investment projects by contributing its own equity or debt financing to the project. The IFC also takes a very active role in the projects it supports, becoming involved in the structuring of projects and sometimes in actually conceiving and designing the projects. In the financial sector, IFC's objective often is the development of local institutions. IFC has a separate department to handle financial sector projects which constitute about one-third of its portfolio.

C. Comparison with Other Public Sector Insurers

To further place the MIGA guarantee program in perspective, a brief survey of other public sector insurers was conducted to collect information on their treatment of financial sector projects. A total of 12 public sector insurers were contacted and they all responded. The results of the survey are depicted in Table 1.

Of the 12 insurers, 10 reported that they support foreign direct investments in the financial sector. Of those 10, half reported a volume of activity of some significance in the sector. The average percentage of those five insurers was 7.2 percent of all projects, with a minimum of 3 percent and a maximum of 13 percent. The two respondents that reported no support for financial sector projects were primarily focused on export credit and insurance activities.

Only three of the respondents reported that they have in place a formal program to measure the developmental effects of financial sector projects and, of them, two do so only at the time of project approval. Four respondents reported that they do not have in place such a program, two reported that they give some consideration to developmental effects as part of the risk assessment process and one reported that it considers foreign direct investments to have *prima facie* developmental benefits.

---

[48] Mr. Wolfensohn went on to add: "I see ... financial sector reform ... as especially urgent and, as many of you know, I am concerned that ... we are falling short. In the financial sector, we clearly need to increase our capacity and expertise, but we also need a more wholehearted commitment in our work programs as to the importance of this area".

Table A1. Results of Survey of Other Public Sector Insurers

Agency–Country	Support financial sector projects	Financial sector projects (% of portfolio)	Measure development performance	Treatment of financial sector projects
OeKB-Austria	Yes	3[1]	No[4]	Equal
OND-Belgium	Yes	0	No	Equal
EDC-Canada	Yes	0[2]	Yes[5]	Equal
COFACE-France	Yes	0[3]	No[6]	Equal[9]
C&L-Germany	Yes	8.8	Yes[7]	Equal
SACE-Italy	No	-	-	-
EID/MITI-Japan	Yes	0	No	No response
NCM-Netherlands	Yes	8	No[8]	Equal
COSEC-Portugal	Yes	3.4	No	Equal
CESCE-Spain	No	-	-	-
ECGD-United Kingdom	Yes	0	No	Equal
OPIC-United States	Yes	13	Yes	Equal

1. Concentrated in Eastern Europe.
2. No exposure of any significance.
3. Less than 1%.
4. Believes it is nearly impossible to measure.
5. As part of risk analysis. Does not compile data.
6. Indirect consideration as part of risk analysis.
7. Initial screening stage only.
8. Considers foreign direct investment as *prima facie* beneficial.
9. There was reluctance prior to 1993 because of perception of higher risk.

The U.S. agency OPIC was the one respondent that reported a formal pre- and post-approval developmental effects assessment process. It stated that it considers primarily direct employment and income generation effects and that, on that basis, financial sector projects lag behind certain infrastructure projects, but are clearly ahead of other service sector projects. OPIC further stated that, even though manufacturing projects tended to be associated with higher direct benefits, financial sector projects were recognized as having significant and beneficial indirect effects on host economies and, therefore, "compared favorably" to manufacturing projects. OPIC also attempts to measure impacts at the subproject level (the projects in the real sector that are developed using the funds provided by the OPIC-assisted financial institutions), except in the cases of general branch network expansion or recapitalization investments where funds are commingled with other funds and, therefore, are difficult to trace.

Nine of the 10 respondents who reported that they provide support to financial sector projects stated that they treat such projects equally with any other projects. (The 10th, a respondent with no experience in the sector, did not reply to the question.)

It is clear that MIGA supports a higher number of financial sector projects in developing countries than other public sector insurers. This is partly due to a higher demand for MIGA's services due to the provisioning waivers often granted to these financial institutions by national regulatory authorities for investments covered by a MIGA guarantee. Also, MIGA's developmental effects assessment process is significantly more involved than that of all other public sector insurers, except for OPIC. This is undoubtedly due to the different mission and objectives between MIGA and the other public sector insurers (who are largely interested in promoting investment by their national investors as a matter of national competitiveness).

IV. A Review of Selected MIGA-Assisted Financial Sector Projects

This section presents a review of a sample of nine MIGA-assisted financial projects that have been in operation for sufficient time to have produced tangible results. All of these projects were part of MIGA's active portfolio between fiscal years 1990–95. Of the nine projects, eight have been evaluated by MIGA staff or consultants. The remaining project has been reviewed on the basis of self-evaluation.

The nine MIGA-assisted financial sector projects evaluated are Société Générale's initiation of full scale commercial banking activities in Pakistan; Citibank's expansion of activities in Argentina and Pakistan; BankBoston's initiation of a residential mortgage facility in Argentina; ING Bank's expansion of operations in Brazil; Crédit Agricole Indosuez's and Bank of America's expansion of operation in Pakistan; ABN–AMRO's initiation of full-scale commercial banking activities in Kazakhstan; and ING's investment in a pension fund management company in Peru.

In Table 2 these financial projects are briefly reviewed in terms of benefits rendered to their host countries which are directly or indirectly associated with the project; these reviews are based on the following factors:[49]

> *Transfer of technology, training and employment*
This factor concerns information necessary to ascertain the expected and actual contributions of the project and any subprojects in terms of transfer of technology and know-how, training of indigenous personnel, and the generation of employment in the host country.

> *Development of capital markets*
This category concerns information necessary to establish the expected and actual impact of the project and any subprojects in terms of the development of the capital markets and financial institutions of the host economy, including the development of new financial instruments, more competitive local financial markets, more efficient local intermediation, and mobilization of local capital, etc.

> *Contribution to economic growth*
This factor concerns information necessary to initially assess, and later measure, the impact of the project and any subprojects in terms of development of the private sector, exports, infrastructure, and other development measures in the

---

[49] The ratings of project impacts in Table 2 are based on qualitative judgments of Dr. Plionis related to what was or could have reasonably been expected to occur as a result of the project.

– 81 –

host country, including backward and forward linkages. The host country's policies and enabling environment are taken into account when assessing a project in order to have a reasonable chance that the linkages exist between project activities and economic growth.

➤ *Improvement in living standards*
This factor concerns the project's and any subproject's contribution to the improvement of living conditions in the country, including environmental conditions and poverty alleviation. It must, however, be noted that financial sector projects do not generally influence living standards directly in a significant way. The focus for these types of impacts must be on the subprojects.

➤ *Consistency with government programs and complementarity with programs of other development institutions.*[50]
This framework element concerns information needed to ensure satisfaction of the requirements of the MIGA Convention with respect to the project and any subprojects. Specifically, this category should include considerations of macroeconomic and other policies affecting the financial sector and any determinations made by IBRD, IFC, other developmental institutions as appropriate, or the government regarding the desirability of foreign entry into the sector.

Table A2. MIGA-Assisted Financial Project Developmental Effects Evaluation Matrix

Project	*Country*	*Evaluation Factor*				
		Tech. transfer/ Employment	*Capital markets*	*Economic growth*	*Living standards*	*Complementarity*
1. Citibank	Argentina	H	H	H	M	H
2. Bank of Boston	Argentina	H	H	H	H	H
3. ING Bank	Brazil	L	L	L/M	M	L/M
4. ABN-AMRO	Kazakhstan	H	H	H	M	M/H
5. Crédit Agricole Indosuez	Pakistan	M/H	H	M/H	M	M
6. Citibank	Pakistan	H	H	M/H	M/H	M
7. Société Générale	Pakistan	M	M	M	M	L/M
8. Bank of America	Pakistan	H	M	M	M	L/M
9. ING/Integra	Perú	M	M/H	M/H	M/H	H

H = High; M = Medium; L = Low

---

[50] Information about the activities of IBRD and IFC in the host countries of the projects was collected independently (primarily from the World Bank's Country Assistance Strategy documents and IBRD project documents) in order to assess the complementarity of the MIGA-assisted projects with other activities of the World Bank Group as required by the MIGA Convention.

V. MIGA's Development Effectiveness

The review of nine MIGA-assisted financial sector projects indicates that financial sector projects have distinct characteristics and generate substantially different developmental effects. For example, the dollar amount invested in financial sector projects tends to be smaller than investments in other sectors; their services are offered domestically. Financial sector projects tend to generate relatively small *direct* developmental effects (employment, government revenues, physical infrastructure, direct exports) and tend to have minimal upstream effects. On the other hand, the impact of MIGA-assisted financial projects on the indigenous financial sector, the indigenous capital markets in general, and on the real sectors tends to be very substantial, albeit rather indirect and more difficult to measure.

Based on the information available, MIGA-assisted financial projects have on the whole been developmentally effective, in some cases extremely so. Some of the projects, such as the Bank of Boston project in Argentina and the ABN-AMRO project in Kazakhstan, are truly landmark projects that will have profound influence in their corresponding countries for many years to come. Most projects have had significant positive effects on capital market development and the overall economic growth of their host countries, and, to a lesser known extent, on their social development.

Complementarity with the policies and activities of development finance institutions, and those of IBRD and IFC in particular, as well as those of the host governments has in some cases been extremely high. In other cases the projects have simply been supportive due to the inherent limitations in the potential of a single project to make a big difference in large and fairly diversified economies. The former cases involve projects that were pioneers in a country or in the sector and they exemplify the type of project that MIGA should strive to identify among incoming applications and assist to the maximum extent possible. Such pioneer projects are also often the ones most in need of political risk coverage. There is little doubt, for example, that without political risk insurance the ABN-AMRO project in Kazakhstan would not have taken place. MIGA's unique and essential contribution is generally acknowledged by investors in these projects and can be assumed in most cases because, effectively, MIGA is an investor's last resort (compared to most national insurers, MIGA tends to be more expensive and more difficult to utilize). It is difficult to imagine some foreign financial institutions expanding their asset exposure in a turbulent country without political risk coverage. However, the value of this role tends to diminish over time if country conditions significantly improve. In other cases, it is quite likely that the need for political risk insurance will persist.

VI. Observations and Conclusions

Financial projects are sufficiently different from projects in other sectors, in general and with respect to their developmental effects. The main contributions of the projects are not in the areas of direct employment or income generation characteristic of most MIGA-supported projects. With the exception of technology and skills transfer, most of the developmental effects are associated with the secondary projects (often referred to as subprojects) that are made possible by the financial resources of the projects (such as mortgage financing and privatization in Argentina, trade financing in Pakistan, development of capital markets in Peru, etc.). Although the overwhelming preponderance of these impacts is evident to project monitors visiting the projects, they tend to be difficult to measure. Where the guaranteed funds are used to support a specific financial product (e.g., leasing, mortgage) or where subprojects can be identified (e.g., ING Bank-Brazil), MIGA is able to better trace the project's developmental impact as these funds affect different sectors.

Information about the kinds of indirect effects more commonly associated with the financial projects are not specifically identified or consistently quantified. This is especially problematic when it comes to reporting impacts of financial projects on the real sector. In light of the above, it should not be surprising, therefore, that financial projects suffer in comparison to other types of projects if the comparisons are based primarily on the direct developmental effects of projects, usually direct employment and income generation.

In conclusion, it seems clear that financial sector development is crucial to the development of emerging economies and that foreign direct investment has a significant role to play in such development. Thus, there is a clear link between MIGA support for financial projects and developmental benefits.

MIGA Member Countries

146 Member Countries as of August 31, 1998

Industrialized - 20

Austria	France	Japan	Spain
Belgium	Germany	Luxembourg	Sweden
Canada	Greece	Netherlands	Switzerland
Denmark	Ireland	Norway	United Kingdom
Finland	Italy	Portugal	United States

Developing - 126

Africa
Angola
Benin
Botswana
Burundi
Burkina Faso
Cameroon
Cape Verde
Congo, Democratic Republic of
Congo, Republic of
Cote d'Ivoire
Equatorial Guinea
Eritrea
Ethiopia
Gambia, The
Ghana
Guinea
Kenya
Lesotho
Madagascar
Malawi
Mali
Mauritania
Mauritius
Mozambique
Namibia
Nigeria
Senegal
Seychelles
Sierra Leone
South Africa
Sudan
Swaziland
Tanzania
Togo
Uganda
Zambia
Zimbabwe

Asia/Pacific
Bangladesh
China
Fiji
India
Indonesia
Korea, Republic of
Malaysia
Micronesia, Federated States of
Nepal
Pakistan
Palau
Papua New Guinea
Philippines
Samoa
Singapore
Sri Lanka
Vanuatu
Viet Nam

Middle East/
North Africa
Algeria
Bahrain
Egypt, Arab Republic of
Israel
Jordan
Kuwait
Lebanon
Libya
Malta
Morocco
Oman
Qatar
Saudi Arabia
Tunisia
United Arab Emirates
Yemen, Republic of

(list continues on the following page)

Europe/Central Asia	Latin America/Caribbean
Albania	Argentina
Armenia	Bahamas, The
Azerbaijan	Barbados
Belarus	Belize
Bosnia-Herzegovina	Bolivia
Bulgaria	Brazil
Croatia	Chile
Cyprus	Colombia
Czech Republic	Costa Rica
Estonia	Dominica
Georgia	Dominican Republic
Hungary	Ecuador
Kazakhstan	El Salvador
Kyrgyz Republic	Grenada
Latvia	Guatemala
Lithuania	Guyana
Macedonia, FYR of	Haiti
Moldova	Honduras
Poland	Jamaica
Romania	Nicaragua
Russian Federation	Panama
Slovak Republic	Paraguay
Slovenia	Peru
Turkey	St. Lucia
Turkmenistan	St. Vincent and the Grenadines
Ukraine	Trinidad and Tobago
Uzbekistan	Uruguay
	Venezuela

18 Countries in the Process of Fulfilling Membership Requirements

Industrialized - 2

Australia   Iceland

Developing - 16

Africa

Chad
Central African Republic
Gabon
Guinea-Bissau
Liberia
Niger
Rwanda

Asia/Pacific

Cambodia
Mongolia
Solomon Islands
Thailand

Middle East/North Africa

Syrian Arab Republic

Europe/Central Asia

Tajikistan
Yugoslavia, Federal Republic of

Latin America/Caribbean

St. Kitts & Nevis
Suriname